FACING THE MONKEY'S GRIN

A metaphorical, meditative and real-life journey into the soul of selling. The misanthropes, or grinning apes, haven't taken over the passion of our human triumphs and failures—yet. But be careful. That smile may just kill you. Good luck. Don't quit. Be good.

I0094182

BILL PEZZIMENTI

Contempo Publishing

Contempo Publishing

652 Hogans Rd North Tumbulgum NSW 2490.
www.contempopublishing.com
Copyright © Bill Pezzimenti 2026.

A catalogue entry for this book is available from the National
Library of Australia.

ISBN (Paperback):   978-1-7643986-0-2
ISBN (eBook):   978-1-7643986-1-9

Cover design and illustration by Rubi Creations Digital.
Internal design by Contempo Publishing.

Printed and distributed internationally by Ingram Spark.
First published in 2026 by Contempo Publishing.

Disclaimer

This book is a mix of nonfiction and fiction, intended solely for entertainment purposes. To protect the privacy of individuals and organizations, the names, identifying details, and certain characteristics of people, businesses, and situations have been changed. Any resemblance to actual persons, living or dead, or to real businesses or events is purely coincidental.

The strategies, examples, and insights presented are based on general business principles and the author's experience. They are not guaranteed to produce specific results and should not be interpreted as professional legal, financial, or business advice. Readers should consult qualified professionals before making any decisions based on the information provided in this book.

For my loving wife, Marouli,

Thank you for your unwavering support and patience over the many years I've spent working abroad. Your strength has been my anchor on this journey.

CONTENTS

INTRODUCTION

Much of this book is written from my personal experiences training sales executives and managers around the globe, mainly in media sales. I believe it is a model and discussion piece for all sales reps, young and old; also, for interested managers and those feckless ones, parading ego-driven human behavior. Let's face it, whatever industry you work or play in, you need to sell yourself to sell anything.

Whether you're selling a service or hand tools or a blue dentist chair, buying decisions are universally competitive, and technology doesn't always reduce or tame it. In the 21st century sales reps need more skills in communication, lessons in ethics and kindness and an unbiased eye for precision and protection. The business landscape is shifting and moving fast like a social media news headline. The old ways of doing things and the untangling of a confused hierarchy may only leave you disenchanted, tired or broke.

Get on board with selling, living and surviving the wild unpredictability in a fiercely disheveled and psychedelic planet. You will find something to keep, that will help you navigate the career you're entitled to. This book is for those committed to building a well-rounded career. It's not just a quick motivational boost but a practical guide demanding consistent effort. Expect to revisit it, reflecting on how to implement its advice and real-life examples, regardless of your experience levels. This book will show universal principles and practices, to guide your career, your decisions and to help you sleep at night, safe from the internal, unobservable battle ground of your self-esteem.

PREFACE

Look me straight in the face and say that again. This time, shake my hand, not my confidence. When you are just chasing money, you shake the trust out of the meeting tree onto the dry earth of cynicism and fading providence.

We want to please! We want to win! We want to be noticed! We are fading smoke swirling around a visual ladder, upward towards perceived success and perceived happiness. We imagine. Customer focus is the linchpin. If you consistently push a personal agenda, be advised you are pushing business out the door. The valuable work habits we adopt should always be perfected, coached and practiced daily. Sales is a full-time, demanding discipline that provides either rich achievement or miserable bankruptcy.

With many of our quick decisions we are limited by time, and the appropriation of that time.

In sales – as with life, love and unexpected pandemics – you must consider the abstraction of who you are to fully connect and respond.

The abstractions are the colors, shapes and collision of lines when crossing boundaries that form, that interpret and reshape us as we evolve or disintegrate.

This book will require you to take stock of who you are, your real self and your real potential—and not be influenced by others who would shape and sculpt a different *you* if they were able to.

We will look at the overcapitalization of your obedience. We will look at your misplaced honor and the respect you bring to your work.

In this book we will see how you can become a noticeable resource to your clients. An authentic asset to your company. A unifier to your family, and truer to yourself. The art of being brave, definably original and exceptionally human, in a complicated, mixed up and sometimes inhumane business landscape.

Not all things work all the time. This is not a panacea for a join-the-dots career or a stressless life with an unsavory boss or company.

There are clues that allow you to navigate your work life – and survive the wild unpredictability – in a fierce career and psychedelic planet. This book is global; it speaks true in many languages. The contents may be heavily influenced by media sales, but these are universal business practices to guide your career, your decisions and to help you sleep peacefully at night, free from the internal, unobservable battleground of your self-esteem. In this book bravery, and how bravery is encouraged and learned, will appear frequently on the following pages.

There will be pieces of many places and good people I have been lucky to meet during my globetrotting media career in radio, print and TV.

It is not one geographical place; it is nonfiction and fiction—but all painfully true. The names have been changed to protect the stupid and incompetent. Most companies are not bad - people will be.

CHAPTER 1

Toxic fun / Players in the sales team.

Welcome to the fluctuating and dynamic world of business. Like an incorrigible child demanding sweet rewards, excitable managers shout threats and innuendos to change your output, their circumstances and your behavior. The deliberate execution of 'push management' (I'm the boss, you're not) is the opposite to open, creative participation. It is an unsound function of a control apparatus used to hide weak and unimaginative management. The gunslinger manager with a nervous grip on its staff rides clumsily against the sunset of a dulled corporate culture. It reveals an inflexibility with the intolerance that is generally a by-product of shaky nerves. Openly unzipped, he or she is shooting up fish or anything that gets in their way. The inauthentic self in a barroom brawl with themselves and their bank account.

Throughout your career you will observe workers toeing the line, believing in the gaminess of their company and its ideals. And they get side-by-side support from LinkedIn and other professional accessories who are sycophantically activated. They are propped on various stages of the organizational karaoke singalong, surrounded within the crowd's earnest followers. Marching along to the social media grand stage, congratulating their networking friends on their accomplishments while spreading advice that has no material or spiritual substance, other than the offering of a colorful emoji or a "you nailed it" as their rallying cry to yours or other groups. It's insipid admiration.

In the sales field it is common for ordinary people with good intentions to band together to form "team jackals", congregating to defend their territory and rank.

I have worked with, and learned my sales craft in media from, wildly brave entrepreneurs and hard-working company leaders who bond well with their employees and the market they serve. I have worked with many 'jackals' as well. Their shadow is larger than they are.

Regretfully, too common in many businesses, the bad and indifferent get promoted, because of tenure, a charming, exaggerated smile or an aggressive too-hard-to-deal-with personality. There are many other untenable reasons why they are picked that have only superficial similarities from a loose benchmark. When hiring, in many cases, it's confidence – not necessarily skills – that enables graduation from mid-level to senior-level positions.

Then there are the "hired guns" specifically positioned to ruin the office fun. The motto from frustrated management is, "Shake up the team! Light a fire!" With no aim or purpose, but to perhaps disrupt a complacent, fatigued team. You know management has run out of steam, vision and resolve to correct listless attitudes when they resort to temporary outside *mobsters* to straighten the bent. I know, I was one.

A 'shoot-out in the OK Corral' is not an ideal motivating tool; as a manager you will be left picking up dead bodies from time to time. Yet, despite the expressionless stiffs littering the hallways, this tactic sometimes results in gruesome "slaughters" that can serve to awaken the comatose habits of the team, who grudgingly adjust—mostly out of fear of dissolution and corporate assassination.

And then there are the 'designer deity' sales reps—the ones always angling to be close to the top apes, picking their brains and fleas. Grunting, glimmering, fucking and yelping their way up the golden ladder. These are the office imposters who will hijack your time and sanity from one episodic drama to the next. Avoid these hysterical and dangerous adolescent disruptors or be prepared to do their bidding, with a tightly gripped hand on shrinking balls. While those at the top of the tree are eating golden pineapples and coriander, they will ignore the ruckus below. It'll go away, they think. It doesn't— it manifests as a free-for-all.

We should look towards building an immersive company narrative that is honest, workable and considers all its people. The content and application with on-going training to connect all levels of the organization, the discipline of no nonsense – especially at the very top – to embrace the same outcome and goals.

There should be greater consistency in actions, and trust of how best to find a higher emphasis on inclusive communication. One that constructs a broader, more equitable revenue stream for all employees, and teaches the potent skill of creative improvisation and how to think on their feet (instead of with their hearts) while at the same time working off an unworkable old script.

We tie our 'self-wagon' to that job post like a fleshly soul that we bring back and forth to work. While carrying a heavy company-logo backpack, drinking tea or coffee from a company-logo mug—all to give us a sense of belonging, value and purpose.

And so it goes – in sales and in life – the operators will punish those that miss the mark of excellence. Especially the fingerless, pointless, spirited monkeys who are easily disturbed by the natural course of business and life that continually flows from calm seas to rocky channels and back again.

In the early days of my media sales career, I worked for a well-regarded radio station in Buffalo, New York with significant ad-spend from major agencies and clients. Outwardly successful, the internal management were abusive and paranoid. I accepted this coveted position only to regret it by the end of the first week. The general manager was a loud, bullying figure starting each day aggressively. At 8 a.m., he would storm into the sales pit like a growling bear, ostensibly to ensure punctuality, but primarily to berate and insult the sales team. I witnessed his menacing behavior, stunned by his unwarranted browbeating of his employees. Later that day I asked the senior sales rep what this was about. He shrugged and admitted: the money was good, he had a family to support, and the station's cool image was appealing, so he just put up with it. To him, the question was puzzling; he saw the abuse as normal. The normalization of a toxic work environment in many cases is the norm. Whenever I question the pervasive toxicity with companies and managers who seemingly need mental health support but persist with out-of-control authoritarian disrespectful attitudes, their response is generally another excuse—one that is seemingly never tied to the person's dignity. Don't let your workplace become your dark room where you will adapt and become desensitized. Give it enough time and this toxicity becomes ingrained in the culture of the company, making it seem normal.

If you find yourself trapped in a highly toxic work environment and cannot afford to leave immediately, here's what you need to do: first, recognize and accept that this environment is toxic and not normal; second, understand that as a single individual you are powerless to change an ingrained culture alone; third, treat the entire company environment as potentially hostile. Keep your opinions private and refrain from sharing them with peers, as they may exploit your words to their advantage. Avoid speaking negatively about the company or individuals at all costs. Lastly, make finding a new job your top priority and mission.

In the face of toxicity, safeguard your peace, stay resilient and relentlessly pursue other work channels. You and your future are worth it. What a comforting bedtime thought. To dream that you have that much control of your life in the 21st century or, at the very least, between 9 a.m. and 5 p.m., Monday to Friday.

There's nothing hidden. There are always witnesses around, both good and bad spirits
                              -Tadodaho Chief Leon Shenandoah

CHAPTER 2

Managers under pressure /
Read the room.

Bosses aren't all bad or good. Many are misguided or shaped
by their experiences, or have daddy issues, or perhaps are
influenced by books they've read, or even being raised in a
culture of strict dogma, which can be difficult to shake. They
carry along with them the friends and acquaintances they have
worked with on their "yellow brick road" career path, to fit
them in comfortably. Although they may not be the best
qualified, they are trusted. In saying that, I have seen a senior
manager groom and mentor such people, only to be stabbed in
the back by opportunity or delusional hubris. The beat goes on
and on. You may also find yourself working for a
temperamental and emotionally narcissistic employer who
will effortlessly dump you for another misguided petitioner
begging for attention and approval. There are thousands of
hungry sales reps out in the cold who lust for too much

attention. The sales world is a place of moving parts turning forward and backwards, from peak performance to burn out.

As a leader there are both slippery and dry conditions that will undoubtedly challenge your patience and authority. Money is the deadliest of all weapons. It's the *hallelujah* in the sermon. It is required, but it is false power. It fades. It blends. It is liquid. It disappears. But money does have a long lifespan when separating the strong from the weak. When it is used to control and delegate—like a gun or a fantastic idea. These days, personal ethics, resolve and market cap are the real power. Corporate titles of importance and influence are confined to vanilla boardrooms, suspended in time like a gallery wall of lifeless corporate headshots that are interchangeable and, thankfully, mostly forgotten. In a melodramatic school-fight moment, a folksy and, seemingly earnest, CEO removed colorful tropical fish from executive offices. This was an act of public contempt aimed at the managers and the entire underperforming staff. Apparently, his disappointment was due to a *slight* decline in the company's quarterly figures during a severe market downturn. The once accepted and now unpopular fish were dismissively tossed by a fish caretaker into a half-filled water pail. (No fish were injured during the transfer; one fish was insulted, but that's all we know.) The vaudevillian histrionics from an enraged, out-of-control leader in full view of the staff could be considered comic slapstick or, on the other side, could lead to the serious deterioration and undoing of a team's trust in leadership. This manager was more interested in the bottom line falling even more than he predicted, without considering how his actions looked to the rest of his staff. This was truly poor form as a leader. By failing the "captain's test" of riding the hard winds with surety and a steady hand, his exaggerated *traipse* was at once both comic and tragic. Alas, the symbolic scapegoating and hysterical bleating began by allowing the snatching of innocent fish out of a narrow metal-framed fish tank, designed specifically for pretentious offices, pretentious homes and pretentious budgets. I wonder what would have taken place if the fish were unassuming bottom feeders. Would they have been left alone like many sales reps who have very little choice but to hunt prospects in the cavity of a dark ocean for their livelihood, selling small, inconsequential deals and remaining mostly unnoticed and left alone by management. All the hands-on deck staff remained mute, heads down and stunned throughout this freakish, yet allegorical, sideshow. He dashed from one sweaty office to another like a superhero chasing imaginary villains and loudly cursing the startled fish for breathing. Acting out Darwin's theory of evolution, and growling at contrite managers for their failures, their pretensions and their insufficiency in achieving an unachievable budget. These budgets being rolled out by overseas straw men, who specialize as generalists, never grasping the integrity of the sales team, their efforts and how forecasted budgets higher-than-heaven, and based on a prayer, would be delivered. Get the picture? At the end of all this, no one was fired, and no one died. Just a few exotic fish relocated, never to be heard from again. What did die though was trust. The trust in management as strong and decisive leaders in stormy seas. The trust in management's ability to maintain confident communication with both superiors and subordinates. Alongside, a strong goal-oriented approach is critical in a rapidly changing sales environment. The chaotic or untrained assumption that everything will fit perfectly within a budget sculpted by wishful thinking, rather than strategic planning, is absurd and inevitably destroys the morale of the sales team and staff who are asked to do the impossible. In situations where your manager shows public, exaggerated and ongoing signs of weakness, there is not much you can do except "observe and evolve". It will change your perspective which is shaped by your experiences, bad or good, by reflecting how you see yourself. Over time this will help you to apply and share the knowledge you have gained in various, perhaps uncomfortable environments, and to develop your strengths and opinions. Don't mirror your manager. To simply evolve as a derivative of a dramatic actor is not a smart path towards professional boldness and truth. Keep mental notes and expand. One day when you are chosen to assume the role of leader you will have the skills and experience to leverage relationships that are positive and genuine.

It's crucial to recognize that managers are fallible; they do not possess all the answers. Often management involves a significant degree of uncertainty and guessing. Here's a thought: to evaluate a potential manager's suitability, it might be a good idea to run them through a game-show-type assessment of their decision-making and problem-solving skills under pressure. This is wildly extreme, but the hiring practices of management needs an overhaul. Ultimately, they are no different than you and me, distinguished only by title and other additional privileges. Absorb. Learn from them.

Let's face it, in the sales business there are common disruptions and rearrangements from internal and external influences. It is the unexpected nature of the pathway toward achievement or disappointment. Therefore, the foundation you build your business upon is either made of concrete or moving sand. If it's concrete, you will miss fresh and innovative ideas as you gradually ossify into a hardened stone buried under the rich earth of creativity. If it's sand, you will easily shift and disseminate with the spreading of borrowed opinion and debris to another's borrowed opinion, without any allegiance to your company's true values. Instead, find the time to learn the disciplined art of mind agility. This will boost your power to transform and keep relevant in an always changing, sometimes irrelevant, world. In addition, it is a good idea to follow an ethical business and personal practice. You will become cosmic, revolutionized by transforming yourself from vulnerable-reactive to recognition-essential. When others fall like bad extras in a war movie, it is at that moment you stand straight. Purposeful. Holding firm to your space and not the loose outer space of others.

To win! To be noticed! To make money! To accomplish these goals, we gloriously dispense our strengths and our network freely, like methadone to a friendless addict. We share our accomplishments like a smug Facebook posting and then onto the next exhibitionist platform for all to admire and comment. Sales at its core is a vulnerable, unforgiving and inconstant profession, like being a programmed hitman for 'Ndrangheta in Naples, Italy.

A regiment of daily health conditioning is the binding glue and bearer of your success. Remaining mentally alert and physically strong for the daily grind of an elastic workday – one that requires athletic stamina and the ability to bounce

back from an off day (or week, month or several months) –
with an aim to push forward each day, and each day that
follows. Now is the time to manage your special life and
mount a rebellion against the soul swindlers

Many of us have worked for promising companies that
have a policy of "open door" management. This wide welcome
door, as benevolent as it may sound, can release debility that
quickly opens to vain favoritism, to you or others within the
company. You are then obliged and well compensated to
prostrate and obey. Not to think. And certainly not to show
signs of individuality. If you are one of the chosen few that are
paid extraordinarily large sums of money, in time it will
increase your inclination towards puppy-like submission,
faithful obeisance and, periodically, grumpy apathy.

The open-door-by-invitation that is rooted more to royalty
and kings than the Western entrepreneurial spirit, does not
necessarily require a special talent or a blatantly convincing
allegiance. All you're asked to do is to become malleable. To
trade self-respect for money. At this table of self-barter and
duplicity, if you freely offer enough noisy *mush* in between the
uncomfortable drinks, you may receive a permanent seat. But
listen carefully in the restless corridors at work. You will hear
the mutterings of discontent from the unchosen, in office
corners and foyer cafes. The envy is weighted heavily and

cannot be avoided - discontent is the mistress to neglect and its brother is mutiny. Humans talk to each other and talk *about* each other in praise or reproach within the openness and shadows of their lives. It is our way of getting garbage out, bonding and seeking validation and support. If you are looking to be right, or perhaps you are frightened of an uneasy internal feeling, there is always someone close by that will offer a shoulder by embracing your one-sided point of view.

Many times, I have overlooked frivolous gossip in the office as being a healthy way to relieve tension or a way to uncover dissatisfaction from those who are not confident enough to endure a different perspective from their boss. Gossip is neither professional nor unprofessional. It's naturally human. But gossip can become defiantly toxic, turning a generally positive environment into that of a negative one. If that occurs, then removal of that person or persons should be quick and final. It does not matter what title they hold or their tenure, they should be discharged. A whisper can carelessly grow into a roar. This needless malicious disturbance is costly to the company and careers. The swift action of a no-compromise removal may look and feel draconian – and it is – but the survival of a healthy office is sovereign. To offer neutrality is to be open to misinterpretation and insidiousness. They are not children. They are not family.

They are adults and employees. Treat each of them equally and respectfully as such.

If the company has built a cracked foundation of greed, preservation and poisonous gossip, you will have to decide how you want to be recognized and how you recognize yourself. The disingenuous part of you that seeks approval or the courageous professional that is steady and straight. Your choice. Or perhaps all your good characteristics that have left you marooned away from your dignity and expression have been seduced and swept away? No choice. A word of advice: being too brave may cost you your job – or worse – your good standing in the company.

Those in sales understand the mental bruising of missed budgets, pissed-off clients and the wrath of mercurial managers who are under even greater pressures: the pressure to please skittish shareholders, the pressure to increase profit margins, the pressure to soothe an incendiary staff—each and all wanting more of your flesh, peace of mind and revenue. Exhaustive, almost fatalistic! Perhaps childishly unfair or unrealistic. Yet it is exhilarating when you hear the united marching sound of a successful company with all parts and players moving as one in the same direction. The French have an apt word for this – *succès d'estime* – which translates to 'success of esteem'. When all employees, regardless of their rank, become the whole of a successful company and are recognized for each of their individual contributions. A place where no individual is left out or diminished by short-sighted, aggressive chieftains, grinning apes or out-of-focus objectives. The great companies that embrace this winning philosophy of salvaging staff, of rewarding effort, of embracing training preparedness and allowing open discourse will achieve oversized success and growth.

Each of us wants to ascend (not just when we die). Most of us work to achieve specific goals, substantiate our dreams, and contribute. We network with others, and their others, sharing a destination with an idea or singalong. We join professional clubs; we follow experts on social media that shape our opinions, from a quickie thought to a lengthy podcast. Some companies hold employee picnics with the usual garnishes of syrupy soft drinks and avocado sandwiches, to find a connection that will stimulate productivity, cooperation among peers and enhance their work behavior. The company is showing empathy by bringing together a complimentary staff in a communal environment.

Regardless of how we digest information or share ourselves, you'll find in time that if you look deep enough you may get past the media clichés and discover there is no such thing as fake media, there is only fake you, and by taking on board the things that drift and are easily consumable, it is like an opportunistic cult preying on the lost and glassy-eyed.

We demand attention! Waving tattooed arms excitedly at an adopted tribal family to secure a spot around the burning-man fire or at the white linen corporate table. We gather truth and misinformation like imported cheese placed in a wicker basket of tasty platitudes. This, simply to pass it along to a network for support and edification. Our first impulse in many unknown situations is to either accept it or reject it in an instant. Introspection or meditation of silence and the sacrosanct internal connections are thus sacrificed. We believe it is obligatory to join a business club, a 'groupthink' society or just play a round of networking golf. It closes in on the extraordinarily little mental space or rebellious freedom of thought we have. The methodology of thinking before you act becomes a clumsy open-mic night, tripping over your soon-dead career in front of a hostile out-of-tune audience.

Look deeper into the company that is led unattended or blindly, without the true values contently patched together by an aped mission statement. And then look deeper into yourself. The meaning is ambiguous. Is it being in a blameful workplace that breeds restlessness and lost potential, or is your restless ambition the source of your lost potential? Questions you will need to ask as you map out your career.

CHAPTER 3

Don't follow. Be genuine.

Social media companies have worked brilliantly in altering our human behavior by collectively elevating and using our voice to communicate to friends, and everyone we know or hope to know.

It's the commercial cohesion, algorithms and obsession to capture our fragile nature, and our simple neediness to connect. And to ensure that the billionaire traders of excess and desolation remain rich. These companies perfectly understand the concept of manufacturing vulnerability and mass loneliness and are making huge amounts of money out of it.

So now let's think about corporate-bongo billionaire motivational leaders engaging us in triumphant motivational activities. Some have borrowed a traditional rite of passage – a test of courage and strength – from Indigenous people dating back to the Iron Age in India: the fantastically-staged fire walk ceremony.

The idea behind putting your feet in harm's way is to capture the power of focus and will by conquering fear triumphantly in front of thousands of strangers. Followers walk briskly on hot coals, which they think will prove them able and capable of achieving great things, all with the power of their mind. This is heady stuff, with a high-ticket price to prove your worth. The heavily produced and directed travelling staged-spectacle show is in front of 10,000 or more white collar followers and believers, in hundreds of Starbuck cities around the world. It is, unfortunately, despairingly fake and easy to accomplish. Walking fast on burning coals will unlikely cause any pain unless you stop for a few seconds to check your Instagram posts or LinkedIn likes.

If they were seriously looking for gravitas in this short form, borrowed metaphor of achievement, the smiling money-spinner motivational speaker should have opted for the sacred indigenous Lakota Sun Dance ceremony. This is where young native men shuffle and dance around a pole in a wide circular motion under a watchful sun. The initiated are tied to rawhide, which is attached to a bone and fastened to their chest, their rhythmic motion lasting for days until it is ripped from their bleeding flesh. Ouch! Now *that's* real pain and spiritual purification, not the pretend suit and tie monetary exhibitionism for the corporate wannabe warriors. And there would be too much real blood and too much crying from the executive class. These kinds of shows provide the followers with a false sense of power and accomplishment, one that tells them they can now achieve anything.

The simple truth is that you can achieve anything you put your mind to (within reason) with a whole lot of hard work. Save your money and put it towards education rather than group-cult exploiters who do it for their fame and your money.

So much more is demanded of each of us in a make-believe world of mistruths, cartoon characterizations, loud sound, fake heroism, distortion and preschool images. A deafening, repetitive piercing noise that obscures truth, intelligent conversation and self-consciousness. We listen to overpaid, sappy laughing from radio and TV announcers, along with their podcaster cousins, spewing inane controversy powered by childish award-winning commercials. All this, plus group boredom, just to grab you by the neck, shake you suggestively, and shape your thinking, desires and experiences. Alice in Wonderland, if anything, is but an active-wear suburban commuter compared to these fantastic characters.

Today, with every mind consuming information at iconic speed, travelling within our brains and bank accounts, we are wired for everything. On top of this, the ever-changing industries demand more data, more research, more proof, and more circus side shows.

Look around you, the media influencers are everywhere – you will see women with lips as big as a Louisiana church congregation by having lip augmentation, adding volume like putting an oversized off-road tire on a Mini. How could we think or be individualistic when we wrap our brain in e-business doublespeak, cartoon images, shrieking sounds, assembly line opinions and political biases, all swirling madly around a teeming mind.

The best way to manage the cornucopia of what seems like unsound ideas and ornamental proselytizing is to acquire the discipline of skepticism. The hustle is real, and it is coming from all directions internally and externally. You will have to sift through the field of bullshit to find grains of truth or anything useful to help expand your knowledge, to become a benefit to your customers and an asset to your personal development.

The numerous sales representatives and managers I have encountered during my travels have mostly exhibited a genuine commitment to their roles. Nonetheless, they often find themselves ensnared in a hullabaloo corporate environment that prioritizes a polished narrative crafted by the marketing department or follow-the-leader cheerleading exercises from highly persuasive shamans and high-level executives. Working across the United States with a few different teams, in different geographical parts of the country, I met some of the hardest working sales representatives I've ever met. I saw the pain and disappointment in their eyes when a piece of business fell through or when an email went unanswered. They were real people with real concerns and questions about their own ability and the casualness of a cynical environment.

How do you do that each day without upsetting the internal nuances of cultish nonsense that compares and suggests that you aren't up to the task? You must take control and create a holistic balance of strategies that has a more realistic representation of the corporate identity you're promoting, so that your engagement with customers is enhanced by your company's brand credibility, and your own personal credibility and trust.

You don't need to be a combat engineer to remove obstacles in the front lines of competitive business warfare—just be genuine, knowledgeable and tactical.

CHAPTER 4

Science and media will enhance
or mislead.

While working in Phoenix, Arizona, I was asked to attend a neuroscience presentation by a national radio content supplier to showcase their "exclusive" neuroscience platform to a dozen or so local advertising agencies. I was keen to hear about the science of the mind and how it now plays out in the advertising industry, for the mind is the piece of the body that advertisers would love to master and control.

The seminar was basically a discussion on our brain's impulses and how neurons function. Neurons are the building blocks of the nervous system transmitting information through electrical signals. Normally the application of neuroscience is applied to treat conditions like Alzheimer's and depression. This seminar was to explore questions about decision-making triggers in the brain, based on short-form advertising copy to leverage advertising dollars spent by companies. To determine if a person's central nervous system will respond and process information like memory and attention better if the information, in this case the commercial, is constructed within anything lower than a 30-second format. Preferably 5 seconds using hand signals. Media was making a huge 21st century leap from analyzing simple demographics to decoding the activities of a brain.

Admittedly I was prepared to enter this synapse festival as a sceptic. It's my fallback instinct. Throughout my sales training career, I would advise the sales executives to remain skeptical, and yet open, in all aspects of their life, but never cynical. The former has doubts and questions to explore; the latter has complete disbelief and will bury all possibilities in a dark hole of distrust and nothingness.

I settled comfortably in the back room near a broken air-conditioning unit. It was summer in Phoenix; it was hot and humid. I had an unobserved view where I could happily, freely grimace while watching the attendees' countenance as they played point-the-thumb-and-finger at their cell phones. The earnest presenter walked confidently to the front and center of the room, holding a slide-clicker device tightly as if she was prepared to trigger an explosive. The first slide went up. Images of grey brain tissue and fish? I thought, this is going to be fun. We were told by the Dr Doolittle presenter that fish had a longer-term memory than expected, and they can retain information better than the cloud in your iPhone. (Okay, I exaggerate, but let's see where this goes.)

According to her officious research company, fish are more intelligent than we ever credited. Fish have a better ability to retain information, including Thai recipes, than humans. My initial thought was why fish retentiveness would have so much significant appeal to advertising agents. I hadn't thought of fish that way. Were fish a new demographic to replace the aging baby boomers? I pushed and dismissed that thought immediately. Baby boomers, as the millennial generation know, are indestructible and will never disappear. Consider the Rolling Stones or Bruce Springsteen.

To be fair to the presenter, I learned there are volumes of credible research that through social learning proves that fish know where to find food. I had a couple of goldfish as a kid and it was always remarkable how they found the tiny wafers I plunked into their bowl. They also can play. I was told in Japan, koi have been known to blow tiny thought bubbles with glee, wisdom and joyful detachment – almost like Socrates did before his execution.

I recovered from my daydreaming and returned to the presentation.

It was repeated on the wide screen throughout the presentation: fish have a 6 month or longer memory span. I realize the cognitive powers of fish were not the main talking point from this lecture. It morphed into theatre/science to uncover a pointed creative argument. It was an entire presentation on a singular, one-dimensional opinion and that is: humans today (thanks to noise, social media and indiscriminate clutter, or simply too many ads everywhere) have an average attention span of 8 seconds or possibly less, especially in the case of those who haven't trained their mind to read books written by Russian novelists. It can become quite a convincing argument if you have teenagers or a screaming narcissistic partner who repeats the same thing over and over again.

The strategy behind this fish exposition, if taken in its commercial context, is the reason why advertisers should consider a rethink with their creative content. Shorten the message! The goal is straightforward: to capture people's attention and ensure they retain the information. Much like a programmed robotic fish swimming through predetermined paths, consumers are enticed to purchase an array of products, ranging from electric cars to electric toilet paper. It's driven by strategic advertising to create a demand for shorter form content advertising. According to the gifted presenter, a few seconds of ad content will make a critical difference. She made this claim before the young people in the audience tuned out and played with, yes, their phones or drifted into youth's aimlessness by retreating into boredom. At this point I began to think the presentation was too long and the cute colorful fish images became boring graphs of sameness after a few screen pages. Then the science kicked in, words like "neurotransmitters", "cognitive responses," and "bodily functions"—it was a long presentation. In fact, the entire presentation became so incomprehensible that an evangelist speaking in tongues would have been considered more coherent.

Here's my take on it. There are truths that are clear, yet obscure, all at the same moment. That is the existential side of thinking and feeling. Attention is at a premium these days in the world's crowded marketplace. It's a commodity of sorts, to find our defining space quickly and softly. Some in the media call this battlefield engagement; others call it over saturation. Just imagine being alone with nothing but your phone and social media. Now, add the entire world—that's where we are now.

Back to the presentation.

It gets weirder. *Inhale*. The "I'm here but not here" coterie were asked to each put on a cumbersome-looking headpiece that looked like a 1930's leather flying helmet with plastic coils on top - I suppose to add scientific plausibility and theatre. It was camp. A giddy prop, as opposed to a working exhibit that would have brought tension and soundness to the passive onlookers, or anyone else who doesn't have the skill set to question something as obviously huckster as that display.

The compliant media audience, each adjusted it on their heads, then passed it on to the next person, possibly convinced it came directly from a lab or a dead animal. As I studied the coordination of the staging and the room, the attendees looked disassociated—like bonged-out stoners at a "show & tell" by a police liaison officer preaching the dangers of hallucinogens and Krispy Kreme doughnuts. I supposed it may also prove that humans are more naïve than fish, especially some in the advertising industry, when there's a free lunch and a sideshow of offer.

Researchers, in collaboration with a savvy media company, skillfully use evidence on fish memory to convincingly support product limitations. This approach aligns with how our minds process digestible information, creating a convincing narrative that resonates with consumers and enhances understanding through clear concise messaging. That is, if you're not a fish, but a floating round-and-round human, living in a comfortable fishbowl with nothing but one rock to circle round and working Wi-Fi. We too will remember things like misplaced keys and what to buy.

It takes on many forms; for example, the digital/social media universe loves to loosely sell "clicks" as proof of performance and activity. That is like saying a blind interior decorator can tell you the color of your room by just being in the room. Relevance and seeing are the muted guest. It's never part of the real conversation or description, or the experience.

The choices we make as humans are anchored to our identity, from our emotions, our aspirations, our religious beliefs or non-beliefs, our free will and on and on, since we stepped out of the womb. Neuroscience is an intricate, evolving and expanding study of our hard-wired brain. A few media companies are bold enough to fit a fluffy "show & tell" presentation in their sales tool kit. It carries fun fuel and some science to persuade a sophisticated global industry that the consumer decision-making machinery can be easily predetermined by using fish memory in an alignment with human memory. However, please do not arrogantly assume that just because you now know your backyard koi is nerd-brainy and that order of greasy fish and chips on your plate may add seconds to your memory, that eating sumo wrestlers will make you stronger or Japanese.

There is more to the consumer than a push-action creative trick.

Psychology, artificial intelligence, research and tribal corporate language will always be used in marketing, and advanced to merchandise the mind by designing an accessible revenue stream based on science, a bit of fiction and chauvinistic ideology.

It is not always the back alley of research, but it can be. It is the sleight of hand of commerce and persuasion, combined. Be cautious of its facility. Be wary of clever vs clever. We need to embrace skepticism of data and what exactly it means when it's delivered to the big spenders of advertising looking to engage with consumers.

Research may be a tight – or loose – association to whatever fits your premise. Tools purposed to convert a platform or to monetize an undisciplined proposition. It is not a panacea for creating robotic deference or influence. Although it is entertaining to learn that fish have a perceptive brain. Wherever you may think it leads you and your company is fine. However, it does one other thing. The soulless, superficial comparisons of marketing trivia that instruct us by invitation will distract and distance us from real experiences. I don't understand how fish repeatedly fall for the hook-line-and-sinker trick given their extraordinary memory and retention as studies show. Perhaps they're more human than expected.

As the attendees unobtrusively left the room, more fascinated by their cell phones and text messages, I wondered if they were now convinced that fish were smart and complex, and a whole new target to pursue. Or that the woke in the room would consider an erudite preppy fish as traumatized the next time they see one lying raw-naked on a sticky block of rice, tied, and train-bound, wrapped with seaweed like a vinegar-basted sex slave. Sushi, anyone?

The advertising world's neurologists and marketing gurus interlock the building chains of the brain to analyze how we function and how we quickly respond to our environment and those ubiquitous commercial messages.

It is not done for any altruistic goal, and that's fine, but rather to get a greater share of their advertising dollars from the marketplace. This is not a judgement of values. It's the commercial cohesion that is its nature for the distribution of wealth and competition.

Psychology imitates artificial intelligence as connected-tissue research. Meanwhile the bongo language is interpreted to merchandise the mind by designing a revenue stream based on adult science (therefore it must be true) and sober deliberations.

It is manufactured to semi-control or modify our impulses. Simple non-thinking decisions which are closest to functional human behavior and choice. Like the lower priced impulse goods you see in the manned supermarket check-out or retail stores, such as candy, snacks, scented candles and copies of Reader's Digest magazine.

That's changed, to a degree. With self-checkout machines, they are now catering to the no-kitchen millennials. Maybe we will see the return of the "cigarette girl" with tray and a synthetic leather neck strap offering snacks, candy, and breath mints to the "I'm in a hurry to get out of here" generation.

To get people to act on the message, unconditionally and fast, it then plays a crucial role in convincing frivolous money to transfer to the solicited (through advertising). It is piously said to the client from the "gospel, hallelujah" sales reps that their message method works on all brand items. This idea of expensive, repeated exposure in political brainwashing figures into how long-married couples over time can eventually resemble or reassemble each other, and that good things eventually will happen if you live long enough. This might happen if the message is repeated several million times – maybe only three times for some – and with or without a colossal discount price point, and let's say, *repeatedly* on social media, radio or television.

With luck, empathy towards the product increases. The same can be said if you are unlucky enough to live in, say, North Korea, with a gun to your head staring at Kim Jong Un on an outdoor billboard, or his omnipresent statue smiling up at your kitchenette window from a polite green park.

It used to be called brainwashing or birth depletion. In social psychology it's called the "propinquity effect" – where repeated exposure leads to a reduction in negative responses, but like I said not in all cases, especially in political partisanship, bigotry or human superiority with or without a gun. Repetition in messaging sells, we all know that, but a good reputation for your craft sells even more.

The inking and online media chain of bloggers, influencers, experts and advocates are in the game for your affection and to have a determined meaningful discussion and relationship between you, your wallet, themselves and their website. One problem! There is no authenticity. Just a lot of stalking and attention seeking on the supplier and receiver end. The career strategists are noisily tapping like a woodpecker, hammering empowerment at your hollow brain. I thought strategy was a targeted action, not an Episcopalian Church membership.

The advertising execs and bloggers are sent out as the polished grifters, delivering the message, the package, the price and the promise – all with fevered urgency, believability and attitude.

Current fashion validation matched with a fusion of banal and an egghead sticky substance. Just enough high-minded scientific persuasion to create arousal and distract us from some greater world activity. Like watching TikTok.

Ethical considerations are paramount. Claims based on neuro studies should be truthful and not exaggerated to mislead for the sake of commerce. Neuro studies do provide a competitive edge and are another tool available to improve a sales strategy, but transparency is the key to maintaining trust in the information you are leveraging.

Neuro studies can be powerful to enhance product appeal. When your company presents studies that analyze response linked to sales-conversion rates, before you become a devotee of any tool management dispenses, ask questions regarding its authenticity to avoid a fictional story line that violates your personal brand and ethics. You bring your reputation with you to whatever company you work for so adhere to truthfulness and avoid misleading customers.

CHAPTER 5

Research - the authoritative shaman.

In today's media landscape, research serves as a cornerstone, establishing credibility and authority through rigorous methodologies and testing. This commitment to science empowers media entities to substantiate their claims, position their product and outmaneuver competitors. With a thick, cohesive glue of outcome that fits the promise, it promises to prove commercial viability. It must, of course, be rendered reliable and worthy of detail and many attributes, carrying a compatible strategy that delivers the promise. The shaman researcher strengthens the seducing of our sensory nature with power adjectives, sturdy graphs, and a slick presentation. It's almost biblical in its testimony, therefore, it must be believable and convincingly valid.

An idea, or marketing reverence prayer group, that decodes the hypnotic graphs and percentages illustrated by a product's divine delivery in favor of – or in contrast to – the counterfeit others that it is competing against, is always popular. But is it real?

It's a spiritual assessment to many in the industry, especially those senior managers who are paid a heavenly fortune to deliver a credible product to the cash-strapped market. They want the research to look good. And they want the statistics on how much their product sold against other brands to look good.

Research is a material tool and should be used as a material tool to generate debate, focus, doubt and discussion. It should predominantly be considered as a rudimentary methodology and meditation in examining the whole puzzle of activity and inactivity, missing pieces included. It is not a one-only method system of blind tribal faith coupled with tradition or mysterious events, but a continuum of controlled focus groups and historical data. It is never finite. It has unbiased roots, but then it is picked, skewed and cleaned, ready for packaging.

In the pursuit of clever manipulation from an "idea tattoo", it is re-examined, published and accepted off another "idea tattoo", then blended to concrete practical applications for the discovery of a new, exciting and more convincing argument, substantiated with unshakeable data as an outreach of the latest findings. If you don't understand this statement don't feel ignorant—its sales research talk.

It is then examined critically by the savvy marketplace of advertising agencies, clients and tiny disclaimers. Its believability is within the whole of the research company's reputation, the agency dogma, and whether it passes as relevant to market usage.

Today, with the mind consuming information at supersonic speed, travelling within our brains and highways, we are wired for coruscation or boredom. The media industry wants more data, more research, more proof, more perforated neurons and more fancy dinners.

All controlled by meddling technology. The high priests and dealers of consumerism use research to tell you who you are, what you should watch, read or listen to, and they follow you like a stalker as they cut through your perceptions and truths. They're looking at you through an exquisitely designed lens to see only the superficial, and not your profound experiences, doing this through the power of internal manipulation, peeping-tom-in-the-bushes voyeurism and control.

From primitive cartoon images selling home and car insurance, or banking products, to a simple child's government directive that will ensure comprehension and retention. Our voice is just a voice of many others collected, processed and repeated throughout our life. The repetition of an idea and a message reinforce the solemnity of belief, trust and action, as well as the message itself and acceptance.

All these gimmicks are a monetary ideology set in fake moonstone by a media-branded marketing sorcerer, having access to vast resources to dress up a shrunken-head product with the aim of enlarging an "anthropological" bank account.

Qualitative and quantitative are two popular expressions within the media industry. As well as interaction, engagement, saturation, extravagant claims, attention, lunch and emancipation of popular culture, etc.—all while advertising a multitude of sameness products to the slovenly masses.

We do not live in a real world. We live in an artificial world of constantly distorted and psychedelic graffiti images, loud piercing sounds pretending to be conversation and yappy, happy animated commercials talking through the consumers. All this and more, significantly altering the way we think, act, feel, chew and vape. All invented by our narcissistic desires and money dreams.

This hyper-claustrophobic and encompassing artificial world of TV, radio, billboards, urinal ads, magazines, X, Google, billboards, Facebook, TikTok, radio, news, rapid-read traffic reports and errant bus drivers, are all mind-boggling distractions initiated, distilled and easily swallowed for ultimately all people going nowhere.

Outside, it's a different story: the well-kempt lawns and sidewalks are silent, prohibitive and dangerous. You see bizarrely-trimmed, leashed, gangly labradoodles bobbing down the street like the manufactured creep-dogs that they are. A lot to take in, the well-researched community ready for the next demographic hullabaloo or neurotic poodle.

Personally, I find research invaluable, but it's also important to know when your brain needs a break; I tend to balance focus with an opportunity to catch a well-deserved nap. Staring at laptops all day numbs the creative connection we seek in our professional vitality. When presenting an idea rooted in well-researched personas, close the laptop. While graphs, charts and animated fonts can appear impressive, nothing surpasses the persuasive power of genuine, relatable human conversation with customers. Prioritize personal connection over technical savvy.

CHAPTER 6

Stay connected with clients.

In essence, while technology offers numerous advantages, the human element in traditional methods still holds significant value in certain contexts, by fostering genuine connections and focused interactions. It also offers you, the salesperson, the opportunity to get to know your client personally, which always help to promote good, long-term business relationships.

In today's business world, where "I am too busy to meet with you" is often heard, you need to be proactive, even brash. Otherwise, you will be relegated to emailing your deck or presentation and possibly never get a foot in the door.

So many times, I've witnessed salespeople when faced with "I'm too busy, just send us an email", obediently press send from their office desk, and then tell themselves and everyone else that they have done all they can do! But that is a cop-out. They may have done just as much as other salespeople did, and if you are happy with that, then keep doing it, but I'm here to tell you that the people who succeed in business, in sales, are the hunters. The ones that go above and beyond the others, in search of what they want.

I know that building a client relationship without an initial appointment is challenging and can lead to being perceived as a nuisance, or pest, rather than a valuable resource.

However, if you're busy preparing a gourmet smashed avocado sandwich or dealing with burnt toast in an empty office kitchen, and then just emailing your proposal, your involvement is reduced to just a click of a button. The client has no idea about you, and you have no idea about your client. Meanwhile, your proposal exists in cyberspace, with your colorful presentation circulating among decision-makers and others. They will judge, evaluate, and interpret it—all without the benefit of your persuasive human form.

This *laissez-faire* attitude from the client will likely become yet another rejection on your growing list.

If the client is too busy with an excuse of being too busy to meet with you, I can only assume their interest in your product is less than marginal, and so are you to them. I will also take another leap by assuming they are not decision-makers in the absolute sense, but again, if you don't push to meet with the client, you will never know either. You push hard for that final important meeting. You should make that your mission.

Many sales reps just acquiesce without fully realising the major significance of their inaction. Each step in sales should be a step closer to a close. What I've witnessed is the standard reaction to an instrumental action that is polarized and has very little to do with controlling the sales initiative from start to finish.

The importance of planning and proactive account management comes first by mapping out a strategy in advance, based on historical data. It will allow you to anticipate the right time to approach the prospect or the client, yielding better results, instead of waiting for the right moment to approach the business.

Okay here's how to do it:

   * Employ a proactive approach from the get-go, envisioning that you will get an appointment with said client, no matter how long it takes.

   * If you get a "no" to begin with, just say, "That's okay, I'll follow up with you in a couple of months in case your situation has changed." (It usually does!)

* Find a reason to drop by the client's business unannounced. Maybe you are in the area and just thought you'd drop in to see what their set up looks like. Maybe you have some insider information, and you are in the area, so thought you would drop in to tell them. Get creative. But putting yourself in front of the client will help, even if they don't want to see you.

* Stay connected and keep trying to find reasons to talk to them or call in to their business.

* Stay informed about their industry/company. This will provide an intelligent approach to your conversations and give you a reason to call on them. The client will also start to recognize you as a valuable resource. This will allow you to offer relevant solutions or highly prized creative ideas that stimulate action towards you and your product. Instead of only waiting in line with your competitors to follow a brief.

* Always be prepared for objections—they are the artery that will flow to the heart of sales. Unblock them with persuasive responses by keeping the momentum going and warming interest.

* Consistency and ongoing engagement are the key to account management.

* Don't wait for a brief that your competitors might also receive. Instead, embrace forward thinking, driven by collaboration, creative ideas and a commitment to standing out as a valuable resource. The strength and magnitude of your ability will be defined with a similar partnership as the goal.

As a media sales representative in US television, I led a specialized marketing team, dedicated to securing the entire advertising budget of our targeted clients. Through exclusive marketing partnerships, innovative strategies and community-focused co-promotions, we generated significant revenue. These strategies were tailored in collaboration with the clients through several meetings.

Our bold approach of requesting 100% of their TV advertising budget was unusual in the media industry. Traditionally, ad budgets are divided based on audience size, with each media outlet receiving only a fair share. However, our strategy defied this norm by aiming for the whole pie, which was considered audacious – even laughable – but driven by client needs. And it proved unexpectedly successful.

We secured commitments from seven or eight major national brands for our year-long program. What set us apart was our guarantee of success, tailored to meet clients' sales targets or enhance brand superiority. Our assets included creativity, relentless determination and an unwavering commitment to our clients' success. Meeting clients in person was crucial to achieve our goals. It allowed for authentic engagement, fostered trust and enabled us to fully understand and align with their needs. Unlike impersonal email proposals, face-to-face interactions facilitated dynamic discussions, ensuring our strategies resonated with their goals and expectations.

There is no sure antidote to getting in front of the client. Clients have become modern mythical deities represented by their weird online avatars. But if you happen to be lucky or blessed enough to talk to their manifestation on the phone, well, be advised to stay away from binary questions that require a simple yes or no. Or any question that will not deliver a meeting response.

Holding steady to an open conversation that is not heavily laden with obvious industry buzzwords, or attributes of your product, is the way to go. Keep the client on the phone for as long as possible to get that meeting, either at their office or an accessible cafe.

This is where preparation before the call is critical to the selling process. The phone is not a selling tool. It is a get-the-meeting tool. Avoid selling on the phone. The temptation is often too great for the eager or novice sales rep but try to stay the course and aim for the meeting. Or at the very least a memorable conversation.

Many media sales reps dodge direct client meetings, following the agency's lead in keeping clients at arm's reach. Agencies often prefer to control client access, prioritizing their own relationships. But you have the power to change this. Don't cripple your selling skills by restricting your exposure to young agency staff. In the following chapters, I will go into the critical importance of mastering client management.

If your skills are honed and you have the patience to actively listen (stop talking), coupled with barroom whiskey confidence, storytelling flair, unique product offerings and prepared responses to likely objections, you're on the right path. But mainly bring along your cat curiosity (I promise it won't kill you). A good sense of humor and interest in their goals—now that is superb engagement! Initial meeting. This is your show! This is your time to build your brand and identity.

CHAPTER 7

You vs. the machine.

Many think the old flip chart from days gone by cannot compete against the well-dressed communication of digital color, animated symbols and sound to incite our interest. Modern technology is, well, modern and so we believe that is what we need to show that we have a worthwhile product. Modern technology has become a powerful and expected device that tells your story—without your presence.

However, by emailing a presentation or offer, the sales executive is making themselves obsolete. He or she does not have to participate in person or even online. Just press the button on the keyboard, cross your fingers and pray that the file you slaved over is opened and read. On top of that, you have just lost another unique benefit of your product—you.

Take my word for it, going "old fashioned" may emphasize a distinct advantage. The text-driven flip chart has proven to be a convincing, far-more intimate and compelling presentation tool because the focus is squarely on the seller, not on the expected manga-like visual Japanese anime. With you in the spotlight it allows for real-time interaction and responses that may lead to closing the sale, rather than the client having time to look over someone else's bright and glittery digital presentation.

By using old-fashioned methods, in person, you become the storyteller. You can tailor the presentation as you go, depending on your client's responses and reactions, making the narrative more human and relevant.

The *sweet spot* is that you must be there to turn the pages, answer questions now and lead the prospect at your pace. Where otherwise your presentation or deck is lost within the dull wallpaper of techno indulgence that becomes a diluted impact of too many soulless images, speaking very little and having no human compatibility or interest outside of its bright colors. And it likely will be deleted after a quick browse.

In all your presentations, whether to an audience of one or 20, you want the gallery to be attentive, curious and engaged with your words and style. You want them to be engaged in you, because you will become their business partner of sorts. Most importantly, you want to ensure they grasp the meaning of your message. You are the visual! You are the influencer! Sell the idea of your offer on your feet – even dance if you like

– but keep the room's eyes fixed on you, not a screen. This is presenting in a performance style—it's real selling and real storytelling.

I repeat, if you can, leave your laptop in the car and bring an unobtrusive, old-fashioned flip chart to the meeting. (If you sell laptops, I'm sure you can improvize creatively with the wisdom I am sharing!) Provide a truly customized experience. I've seen too many presentations that were just cut and paste, where the only original element was the customer's name inserted.

The meeting needs to be about your client—what they need and how you can help them get it. It is not about how "cool" your presentation looks. Your sales proposition will complete your individual sales persona with a greater chance of connection and remembrance.

It's important to raise your status by insisting that your presentation gives your company a stronger identification that is robust and sculpted to interact with an offer, by you being the center stage of discourse and engagement. When you move around the room, the room follows. You want the client's attention on you, not on a small thin-sounding laptop. The flip chart is old-school-effective, personal and intimate. If you really want to get connected, get human. It's the best process in sales, integrating your offer while preserving and assimilating a business construct that is far more personal and confident. You need to excite interest, not just present data. You spent too much time building a sales platform to watch it dissolve with the press of a button.

In the following chapters we will explore strategies for securing those hard-to-get appointments, when prospects insist on receiving the presentation via electronic platforms.

CHAPTER 8

To thine own self be something.

Managers of sales reps – I'm talking to you. How about teaching your sales reps the art of selling? Or is it considered too time consuming or too costly? Instead of active training, you substitute titles freely and excessively distributed, much like Oxycontin, to an ill-equipped sales representative or manager hiding behind the shield of a prestigious title.

A dentist's job is clear and well defined. We all know what a dentist does and how crucial they are when we're sitting in that mint green reclining chair, nervous about a procedure. Patients know exactly what dentists do, which is why we seek them out for toothaches and other dental issues. Their offices are busy with aching teeth, bleeding gums and fillings waiting to be repaired or replaced. They aren't given grandiose titles like "Director of Stomatology" or "VP Mouth Executive", although titles like stomatologist are used in some places like Afghanistan. Here in the western world, they are simply called dentists. This title clearly distinguishes them from other professions, like a street cleaner. When you need your teeth cleaned you don't go to a street cleaner. It's essential to know who is qualified to assess and treat the problem.

For evidence of this perceived discrepancy in roles and titles, just visit LinkedIn. You'll find an array of embellished titles like Creative Problem Solver. I'm not sure exactly what that means but it may have something to do with being creative when you're solving problems, or the creatives are being a problem. There's Relationship Manager, which sounds like something you might do in the bedroom. One of my favorites is Creative Shepherd, or any title containing "Guru". One is pastoral and the other is deity leaning. An Account Manager could also be perceived as a person who manages the accountants! And who the hell knows what a Business Development Manager does? It doesn't sound like anything to do with sales.

Some in sales add terms like "marketing" or "leader" to their titles for style and *oomph*. Others follow "sales" with "executive" to convey greater authority. It's mind-boggling that the word "sales" could be considered inferior. It speaks to how sensitive we are about business perceptions.

Apparently, these are all the same job role. Or are they? To people outside of sales, they are complicated titles that force them to ask if you can help them with sales. Because when people want to buy something, that's who they are looking for—a salesperson.

However, many sales reps I've spoken to feel that the word "sales" diminishes their stature within the company and with customers. But why?

The more grandiose job titles allow a privileged majestic outfit to your role. I understand how this perception works. It's more than a hint about how we look at ourselves or hope to be viewed. The company you work for may see this "name fiction" as a critical piece of the business puzzle of opening doors. Yes, business is about power, titles and influence. Titles network smoothly through the labyrinth of who is important, who has value and who is a dud.

But these pretentious and skewed titles are only good for helping you manage some positive self-esteem at dinner parties or a date with an attractive future partner. It seems like it has a lot to do with personal recognition and human hierarchy.

As a stand-alone, a title is simply an empty vessel if there are no competent and passionate activities behind the routine of your work—signifying what you really do and who you are in life. If you are all self-proclamation and title with little content, experience or persistence, then you are a fake. If the management at your company are still wanting to use these silly titles, you may find that they also are hoping that fancy titles will do the selling for you.

As I said earlier, sitting in your office won't always get you the appointment. So too, having a fancy title won't help you get the sale.

The title will represent the speed of clubhouse believability in the "big dog" decision-making acceptance and process. Just like a high-ranking title can get you into the major league of meetings with ease, as opposed to calling yourself an ordinary desk clerk or a simple sagging-pants salesperson.

Kings dine with other kingly types, and your mother's ass is melting. Two realities.

This we know. We are mere mortal sales reps left to play ping pong in a corporate tennis club, if we are not appropriately decorated or assigned a flamboyant title to impress.

I know a CEO (owner of the company as well) who never understood the need for titles. He scoffed at the idea. I reminded him he was the owner. As owner you will and can act like the neighborhood dickhead, and people will listen reverently and obediently as if you just conducted Mahler's Ninth Symphony in the nude. So, it is likely he doesn't need a title; he never had to position his head up anyone's ass (well, maybe one or two bankers). He was the chieftain with the biggest stick, brandishing it for all to see.

I do think everyone needs a job title. It should go hand in hand with their job description, one that they get upon commencement with the company and perhaps gets altered as time goes by if their role changes. But if you are a salesperson, with the responsibility of selling your product to clients, your job title should reflect this. Something like Sales Representative is totally old fashioned, and yet perfect. Be proud of this identity within your company. And if you want the word "manager" in your title, work hard and smart, study, and become the "sales manager", like your current boss, the supervisor to the sales representatives.

Other identity lifters are the clothes you wear, the luxury car you drive, and prestigious golf memberships. These attachments are used to display your influence, your potential success, your symbolic power and who you are and where you sit at the corporate dining table. Though thankfully it is becoming less important in today's business community. That's a good human way forward, yet these worthless attachments are still prevalent in gracious and not-so-gracious societies around the world. If you have a sense of self, it is generally crass and insecure to display your designer success like a bossy baboon, displaying its big colorful ass to the nose of egalitarian squirrel monkeys.

Shakespeare in his brilliant play "Hamlet" wrote these reflective words: "To thine own self be true". My interpretation has always been straightforward, and I generally sided with the literary experts, like my high school gym teacher. To me it's an expression that means simply: be yourself and don't do anything that's outside of who you are. To pretend to be someone else will likely result in failure, disappointment and sometimes, desperately, suicide.

The fake you, the fragile superego that is aligned from a borrowed persona, will take you to the dark side of your soul and leave you there if you're not careful. Unfortunately, sales as a profession is a comparative industry. We look at what our peers are achieving, the money they're making or not making, the haunting whisper of "you're only as good as your last sale". But that is not true at all. No one sells to anyone every time.

So, be proud of who you are and what you do. You sell things. You help your customers. You keep their business running by supplying the products or services they need. Without you and your products, what would they do? A sales job is a great job, and it's important. Your title doesn't need to be complicated.

The reserve of commerce is a delight to behold. It is complete with graceful cheetahs, noble elephants, sociable flamingos and treacherous apes, all moving in synchronicity with the rhythms of the bongo marketplace. A ballet of discourse in a surreal LinkedIn jungle abstract.

I will say this, though, the benefits of thoughtful study, humility and useful knowledge will surpass the forgery of a title with no backbone or experience. Remember, titles carry little weight unless you have "owner" next to your name. Then you can scoff and pretend all you want.

Ongoing sales training – not flashy titles – will elevate your skills and confidence, secure meetings and boost your performance on the sales scorecard.

CHAPTER 9

Burn down your office and greet the day.

If you're not serious about a career in sales, you might only show up to the office a few days a week, spending your time sitting in front of a device, checking emails, browsing the internet and making a few casual calls to client-friends. I call this "nothing time". Some may see it as loitering; others might consider it a waste of time. It will provide you with something resembling a modest salary. The "nothing" replaces a potentially robust day with being or having nothing. You channel Sartre as your work transforms into an exercise in existential futility. Look around your office, you'll know who they are, instantly. Comfortably free riding the company while softly stalking a prospect's website for morsels of more "nothing".

There's exceptionally little benefit for the monastic, candle-burning sales rep – a frozen face carved onto a monitor like lover's initials carved in a tree. There are some sales reps who are quietly spoken, still like a painting, in the library sales pit.

When I accepted a role as a national sales director, I acquired three sales reps on my sales team. In our first meeting they each were quick to tell me they despised the idea of leaving the office and selling outside in Sydney's cold winter. All three preferred to work by phone or on a computer in their candle-burning office, patting their cat's head. Yes, they had a cat too. And yes, a scented candle burned gently on a small, clutterless desk.

Imagine an aromatic Sydney office where gentle incense curls along the walls like Devi Saraswati, the Goddess of Dance; while soft, chilled electronic music pulsates through the erotic atmosphere. On one pristine white wall was a motivational poster depicting healthy young climbers on Mount Everest in shorts; their Ray Bans reflecting stress-free smiles, and on another, a poster of a tiny new-growth pine tree overshadowed by a giant pine with the caption: *DETERMINATION*.

All this promise and calming inspiration in an office with breathtaking views of glittering Sydney Harbour and the gloriously bold opera house. The mascot for their dreamy sales habitat was a sleepy tri-coloured cat who occasionally bounced and purred. This annoyingly nurturing sales office maintained a peaceful mindset but felt more like a house of worship for a neo-pagan ritual conjuring than a reflection of hard work and purpose. Why the hell would anyone want to leave such a meditative, luxurious holy place to go outside to meet an oafish prospect in the hyper-retail game of advertising? I totally understood their sentiments and felt a tinge of envy on how these ladies created this peaceful sanctum. It was my first day in Sydney as the newly appointed national sales director. The pressure to revitalize a rapidly declining new media format was immense, compounded by the recent departure of two previous national sales directors in quick succession. I had to rebuild my entire sales staff from scratch.

One of the three lovely acolytes, who assumed the leader role, wore a loose, longish floral skirt depicting, I think, sunshine and earth. In a firm but soft voice she reproached me for suggesting she should go out into Sydney's cold. It was far too uncomfortable and crude. Besides, sales was an invasive industry and offensive to her abilities as a telemarketer. Adding "she never liked sales". Unbelievably, she said this to me. I whispered to her, "Uh, sorry, but I'm afraid you're *in* sales." Her former NSD, who she believed was wrongfully fired, was apparently much more enlightened than me in every way. This woman told me how the former manager allowed them personal space and freedom to do their job as they saw fit.

They believed they were successful; the company didn't. I believed the company.

Something was about to happen. For a moment I thought I was hallucinating from the stress.

This well-spoken, illogical person said she would prefer to wait for the phone to ring. Her logic on this point, which you couldn't flaw, was that if they called, they were interested. I carefully reminded her that we were in the business of sales. I also added that our office phones never seemed to ring, either instinctively or without being aided.

I had no choice but to hold my position and do what I was hired to do. I proposed another unconventional career path for them. Her steely, loathing gaze pierced through me, as if I were an outdated, bloated V8 engine amid EV's on Interstate TreeHugger.

I imagined being ripped apart and bloodied by hungry pint-sized purring cats, scratching my visionless eyes out while the "good earth" sales team stuffed poisonous mushrooms down my throat, kicking me barefoot in the balls. Just like what happens with most firings.

I refreshed my thoughts to get back to business. I took a bigger leap to break the news to them once again, more forcibly than the last time. I repeated that sales require an enormous amount of outdoor activity, and that I didn't mean hiking through scenic mountains, like their powerful posters projected. No other words were spoken. Abruptly she turned away to go back to her sanctuary. This really happened.

I went to my office, worrying about ordinary middle-class life, floating assets, Bible studies with Satan and the Fair Work Ombudsman.

As it turned out I didn't have to worry about legalities, imaginary hell or physical injury. Within three days all three ladies happily handed in their immediate resignation and left the sanctuary/office, carrying with them scented candles, Buddhist prayer beads, purple crystals, two posters under arm and a cute little tri-coloured cat with his head bouncing to the rhythm of their carriage. I swear they were all humming "You Make Me Sick", by Pink or maybe "Advance Australia Fair".

I was ready to build an authentic sales team.

The previous managers who hired these individuals did so without providing a clear job description. This was expected, given that it was a new startup media company in the market with limited financial resources to hire common sense. They hired people who mostly looked presentable and that were willing to start at the bottom.

During the hiring process, I interviewed candidates from various industries and backgrounds. Many were eager to leave dead-end jobs, even if it meant risking entering another one.

The interview process was gruelling because I was expected to hire talent for peanuts. Our company needed to hire professional sales representatives to fulfill our market promise of being a long-term player, with experienced representation that would provide a strong business foundation. The question that reverberates from any business standpoint is why you would hire a sales team that will likely fail.

New or startup businesses need experienced and proven salespeople to guide the business and get if off the ground quickly. When they have a good team in place and the business is cemented in the market, they can take on less experienced staff, to fuel growth. The foundational staff can then take on the role of teachers within the company, also giving them higher responsibility and job satisfaction. The company will also have to pay these experienced people a little more – they are doing more now – but so be it. If you pay for monkeys, you get peanuts!

I had to convince the founders of the company that to retool the entire sales operation and bring on board real talent would require more cash and a commitment to high standards.

This was not going to happen with just giving high wages to well-dressed men and women, but a focused strategy to build effective sales performance. Higher salaries in sales often contradict growth objectives. For a relatively competitive newcomer in the market, the growth potential is virtually limitless. A startup with adequate financial backing is ready for success from the outset if we develop a sales culture that endorses the business of selling, on-going sales training and sales representation that connects with clients and agencies alike. Sales individuals that practice the art of building client relationships.

By hiring strong revenue generators and offering an attractive commission package, your company is more likely to thrive; otherwise, chant Hare Krishna, buy a cat and pray that your phone rings.

CHAPTER 10

Try to be creative in a creative industry.

Whenever I'm sent overseas by a CEO to assess a sales team delivering unimpressive numbers, I know what I'll encounter even before entering the sales pit: the dull thud of routine that stifles creativity and exploration. It's like the contrast between a noisy classroom and a quiet one. In the noisy classroom, students are engaged, with a teacher who thrives in a lively environment. In the quiet classroom, the focus is on discipline and conformity, rather than on productivity. If the company you work for, especially in sales, demands a solemn disposition, you become a cog in the machine, regurgitating the uninspired status quo that leads to mediocrity. We need creative, adventurous sales representatives who view the marketplace as an exciting opportunity. Too many people in sales spend their career focused on discounts and bonuses instead of generating innovative ideas to inspire.

As part of my observation, I'll instruct the manager to have the sales reps turn off their computers for at least an hour and join me in the boardroom for an open discussion about sales, clients and the challenges posed by advertising agencies. The goal is to stimulate their minds, encourage creative thinking and suggest ideas that challenge conventional approaches.

This exercise typically involves 30 minutes of constructive venting and developing solution skills. Afterwards, I'll encourage them to take a walk, get some fresh air and clear their minds. Numerous studies suggest that our rational decision-making ability is impaired when stressed and confined to rigid structures.

By the time they return to the office, I hope they'll have fresh perspectives and more intuitive insights into the day's demands. Ultimately your success will be defined by the habits that makes you productive and less stressed, rather than sitting stagnantly in an ergonomic chair. So, make some noise and embrace change. Creativity brings a sense of excitement in meetings and in the office. A quiet office is like a library where everything is still and reposed. It is not exactly an environment of spontaneity and the generation of ideas. If people are tripping over each other to speak it is because there is passion and some good stress, but most importantly there is activity.

Creativity is opening up to all possibilities and not by being self-conscious. It's being goofy instead of staid. It's bringing the child inside you to the forefront and letting it all hang out. In business, many times, we take on the persona of "serious" because that that is what we believe to be the persona of an adult or a professional. Creativity has no time for excuses that pretend or ideas that remain idle inside. We are all creative individuals. Our self-talk of not being creative is like wrapping wax paper around a diamond preventing light from shining out. Ideas come from chaos and noise, unexpectedly and unrehearsed. Go to any formal business meeting and you will see mummified attendees who wish they were somewhere else. The freedom to be creative should be the first objective of any meeting that requires input, and the way to do that is by accepting the energy of the room, and that the energy may sound like noise, but it is actually the soul speaking with joy and interest. A sombre and organized meeting room is a creativity killer.

CHAPTER 11

Office politics and monkey meetings.

I was a fixer for an Australian media company. Whenever my CEO felt a market, local or international, was struggling financially, yielding substandard results, or if the manager was acting irrational, he called on me. This wasn't fun work. In fact, it was lonely. My role involved disruption from top to bottom and reconfigurations that would make a mask seem real. Often it felt isolating rather than enjoyable. I never had a permanent office or place within the company, as every assignment was temporary.

This impermanence, whether in the physical setting or work-related friendship, did allow me to maintain objectivity and avoid political entanglements or friendships that might skew my judgment. However, it also meant I had to tread carefully around those with deep ties to senior executives and board members, as their influence could dismantle my efforts.

Balancing neutrality while ensuring effective disruption demanded a nuanced understanding of workplace dynamics and a deft approach to diplomacy. Although, I wasn't always diplomatic. Sometimes impatience got the best of me. At that point of the company correction, I didn't have the luxury of time or a monk's perspective.

The role – or the free will of accepting this role – required me to rely on intuitiveness and navigate consequences from both the staff's "stuck in the past" culture and the acceptance of change for the sake of the company and their careers.

Corporate hierarchy is like a jungle, with spider monkeys swinging effortlessly through the ranks and territorial silver back gorillas slapping trees and asserting dominance, leaving diffident apes in awe.

A jungle it becomes, when livelihoods and self-esteem are threatened by one person who represents the closet decision makers. Many of the salespeople I spoke to had had a long history with the company and seemed to be respected in the industry. They were mostly uniformed, straight-up-and-down professionals working as best they can in a viciously competitive environment. I never blamed these sales reps for the slide in their business because often they were products of inept management and weren't told when things were bad.

In some cases, the reps with tenure had little interest in change if they were on a very comfortable income, not based on productivity, but more on history and friendships within the industry. They would have the least interest in sales training or breaking from their routine. Complacency can look industrious when you bring home a substantial amount of earnings.

There are good reasons why companies fail. The first thing I would assess is the development and growth of the sales team. Many cultural and self-interest beliefs contribute to this failure. A company, in its entirety, can profoundly affect the slow or fast growth mechanisms. For example, it's generally the sales department that generate revenue, other sources for a company to expand can include service fees, licensing, expenses, optimizing pricing, expansion into new markets and leverage upselling; overall, the model for most businesses and key players are in sales and strong marketing. You can see then why a well-trained, motivated sales team is critical to the lifeblood of a company. Any company who doesn't invest in their sales department is rolling the dice, gambling with the future of everyone who has an interest.

To me it's ludicrous to watch how little is achieved with anemic weekly sales meetings that do nothing but examine an intimidating spreadsheet of little value. When a manager's patience is at its peak, which is usually every day, they will sloppily move clients from one sales rep to another quarterly, if there is no activity charted from the original move. It's like arranged marriages – "sisterwives" – to one person in Utah.

On top of that impulsive reaction, hungry or unethical sales reps will fabricate and claim they have a relationship with this or that client, which further complicates the situation. Especially if a sales manager is weak and confused or leaning on poor management practices. A simple solution is to invest in meaningful sales strategies before any shuffle takes place, where managers should collaborate to help their sales reps cultivate genuine relationships. This is especially important considering the ethical implications for commissioned sales reps. The abrupt reassignment of clients can severely diminish a rep's earnings, often due to hasty or poorly informed managerial decisions. Such actions can devastate the productivity and self-confidence of the affected sales rep. I have often seen this happen in organisations that claim to be professional yet inflict unnecessary long-term financial damage because of favoritism, nepotism and deceit.

A motivated and well-trained sales and management team is essential for a company's success. Shifting clients between sales reps undermines the potential for genuine relationships with clients. Although it may sound logical on paper, in practice this strategy acts like a broken back in the anatomy of a sales structure, unless the incoming sales rep has a strong preexisting and personal connection to the client.

I've witnessed situations where sales reps are hired solely because of personal relationships within the industry, mistakenly considered an advantage. The practice is both unscrupulous and unprofessional, yet it often goes unaddressed. The jungle in sales bungles along.

In my history of attending sales meetings, regardless of country or culture, I witnessed countless instances of gatherings that followed a "probe and defend" agenda.

Probe: "Who are you seeing today and what business are you bringing in?"

Defend: This involves fictious meetings alongside real ones with embellished numbers.

These types of non-learning meetings are generally a waste of time. It imagines that there are no other topics to discuss to inspire a likely-bored sales team. Any kind of probing should be done individually in the manager's office, for a realistic assessment that will be made without fear of judgment by everyone in the room. This way you're not embarrassed to show your peers you haven't changed your underwear. It's a stripping down of dignity and confidence for all, including the person who is heading the meeting

A group sales meeting to heighten skills, employ enthusiasm and relevance should include the following:

1. Sales and client training
2. Role-playing
3. Open discussions on current market trends
4. A focus on client problem solving and intel
5. Updates on general product information

This will make the room lively and engaged, and the team will be better prepared by being up to date, and able to answer tough questions in the market within a constantly shifting business environment.

Sales training goes beyond rote learning. It builds an inner strength and confidence within a steel wall of trust between the company, the manager and its sales team. This activity of learning illustrates that the company is enlightened, sure-footed and believes not just in commerce for the growth of the company but also the growth of the individual. Sales tools, sales kits, product decks and research are part of everything that establishes your believability in the marketplace... it should be relevant, cutting-edge and updated to provide an articulate conversation with the client. Sales training outside of the physical tools is holistic and internal. It's personal, in that the lifting of "conscious inertia" will help you become aware of professional stagnation. Helping you move forward to create change without it being forced upon you. It's about breaking free from tedious habitual patterns or procrastination to inherently help make conscious choices and taking purposeful action.

This is applied to spiritual growth, professional development and creative processing. Sales training, if done right, can facilitate progress and innovation. It fosters leadership and the ability to adapt to change.

CHAPTER 12

The phone, the human experience and disconnecting.

While in Toronto, an experienced sales representative approached me in my temporary office for advice on securing a client's contact information. Despite her professionalism and determination, she struggled to identify the marketing director of a key company. Her diligence, evident in client meetings and office interactions, was overshadowed by her frustration with technology and the growing remoteness of the media industry. A likeable, industrious professional, she found herself blocked from simply obtaining a name, let alone a phone number. She'd resort to emails and googling the company's information, even assuming the director was male, all without success. As the weeks went by, I also learned she had other talents like carping and complaining about computers and client's reliance on emails and social media to establish connections. I listened carefully. She blamed

75

technology and how business managers are becoming more remote. All true but at the same time it shouldn't have prevented her from simply trying to work angles within a system designed by humans.

This "can-do" person saw no wide open or narrow passage in obtaining this client's contact details. It was not a business meeting she was chasing, but simply a name and, if lucky, a phone number. I asked her what she had done up to this point to track this needed information down.

She said to me, earnestly, that she had sent numerous emails. Already I'm thinking this is sounding passably futile with the adjective "numerous" and her quickened breathing, sounding more like a dead-end street than a busy corridor. She immediately added – to comfort my quizzical face – that she also googled the company to find his title, as though to prove to me, and herself, that she went way above and beyond the norm in modern communication to secure this person's name and details.

She was unsuccessful. That is why she came to me with her misery. She showed agitation during our discussion, and I knew in a deliberate way I was being tested to come up with a quick, doable solution. My title, tenure and business in her country suggested that I should have an answer or a few tricks up my sleeve or get the hell out of Canada.

Her face expressed an unusual skepticism and frustration, which was unexpected coming from a mostly positive person; a twisted form of what could be perceived as not really giving a fuck or having given up.

Her throaty articulation and modulation were like someone blowing into a moose-mating call horn. and getting nothing for their effort, but a thumbs up from a passing white-tailed buck, who just happened to be wandering the chilled and shadowed streets of Toronto.

I then asked her what I thought at that moment was an obvious question, one that didn't require years of experience, practice or wisdom.

I responded thoughtfully, "Have you tried picking up the phone and calling the company? They do have a general information phone number."

She was taken aback, frozen in a cold Toronto lake of uncertainty. She proceeded to answer with a muttered "no". Her eyes gazing down as she appeared to be having an embarrassed reaction. I could tell by her expression and lack of gratitude that she wanted me or her to quickly disappear. I mean how old and unsophisticated of me to suggest to a millennial that they use the phone.

She went back to her desk – I assume to get reacquainted with her new-found device – and to meditate on how she missed something as obvious and accessible as a phone. She finally did make that call and received the information she wanted. It took her a few months before she asked me another question. She wanted to know what kind of coffee I wanted from Tim Hortons, best coffee in Canada. Several months later we passed each other in the office with heads down and just nodded, as if we had just finished awkward sex. I never understood how and why she missed the phone as another tool to make contact, by mobile or landline.

You just may find you get to the source faster, and you will not have to sit on your exaggerated ass facing a disappointing laptop staring at pixels, waiting for the phone to ring or anticipating an iPhone alert acknowledging that you exist.

If your combative "selling weapons" are simply annoying derivative emails and your newsfeed full of favorite influencers, or you have a compulsion to open Google, LinkedIn or Instagram every 5 minutes at work, then you will become an extremely lonely, ineffective person whose best tool is distributing dry cupcakes to indifferent clients, just to get out of the office.

I would suggest that you go on a didactic holiday with your best friend or attend that never-a-dull-moment two-day software sales training course you've always wanted to take from a CRM monkey. Otherwise jump off your programmed treadmill by teaching yourself to think, breathe and sell instead of run. Learn to be expansive, curious, and simple by being bold enough to pick up the phone and talk to someone. Everyday strangers, friends, family and lovers do more meaningless messaging than talking to each other. We are becoming apes with the inability to construct and relate words that are rich, from a voice that carries weight and real sentiment. It's no wonder we're afraid of A.I.

I've said this many times to my teams—how I crave genuine conversation amid the digital obstructions and noise. You know the kind of raw chat that only comes from face-to-face conversations. Instead, we are in cartoon land, confined to screens of emojis, memes and pinging texts, demanding our attention and "likes". How can we feel the rhythm of a conversation or a powerful message when we're mostly stepping on each other's toes while doing the business dance on a screen.

We send quick replies, scroll aimlessly looking for a treasure or someone outside of notifications, anyone. We are left feeling empty by all the scatterbrained apps and platforms, supposedly created to make our lives easier and more complete. Pick up the phone. Every day you should critique your communication habits – its strengths and weaknesses –

by upgrading your determination to become more intentional and bolder. You may discover that in selling there are meaningful connections if you break bad habits of conformity. Choose courage over convenience with every action you take.

CHAPTER 13

Sales tools - and your mother loves your resume!

Sales is a perilous blood sport, rewarding yet always dangerous. Why? People enter sales driven by confidence, connections or a lack of alternatives. It's a warrior's arena—a limitless coliseum filled with predatory lions, in-heat tigers, silly monkeys and strutting peacocks. Here, every encounter is a battle. We dress to conquer or be conquered. If we don't win, the goal then is to emerge less bloodied than our competition.

We wear the suit of armor (dressed for success relevant to our pay scale or taste). We carry weapons—a long-winded sentence, a quirky colorful marketing presentation piece with pictures or a nonsensical rationale by a marketing GOAT (complete with a degree in "Irritating Clients" from *Bubble University* in Southern California).

What is missing in this contestable and action pack environment?

* The sales skills and articulation to persuade, debate, allure and deflect!

*The courage training to merge honest, pragmatic techniques for engagement and results!

*A client-focused proposal that is relevant to the client, not a generic hand-me-down!

* A black belt in jiu-jitsu for desirable influence and your good health, if all else fails!

While we are performing for the company and the audience in the coliseum, it's necessary to bring these weapons:

* Business logic—not overly used clichés and false promises!

* A considerable amount of passion—not rote!

* Personal and professional credibility—not cupcakes and free lunches!

* Honesty and bravery—not a rehearsed excuse or an unnecessary discount!

Many sales reps in the field lack the necessary tools to achieve even a semblance of success for a balanced livelihood. They find themselves overwhelmed at one company, only to move on to another. With their outdated strategies and aging BMW's, they search for a new place to find refuge, only to often face failure again. Reviewing resumes often reveals a series of life setbacks and bad fits – laid out as though they are accomplishments. I don't trust resumes or any of the latest psychology designed to test potential employees, but which really only serves to expose a mere *tease* of what an individual can accomplish within a fixed environment. The work environment, not the person, may be the pathway to the problem. For example, I know a rep who flourishes in an uncontrolled and free-form environment. Give this person a clock to follow and specific instructions on his daily work habits, he will fail. On the other hand, if I establish invisible boundaries by giving him achievable, but tough, goals and personal trust, I will see him excel every time.

There are others who never really enjoyed sales, and once they are removed from that environment, they often materialize almost out of nowhere, reborn and waving an online 90-day-course certificate as a life coach, a flavor-of-the-month consultant or a startup podcaster. The gilded playful are fascinating (you know their names) as they will twitter all day long like noisy white bellbirds in the Amazon, mesmerizing themselves and their dozen or so impressionable followers with "likes", comments and borrowed platitudes from failed real estate agents drinking champagne at an empty housewarming party.

I suppose it is far safer to play the game when it is surreal or playing pretend or is behind the curtain of failure. Failure, like success, is a pejorative accident in our lives, akin to the crumbling of a marriage or a sudden illness, disrupting our comfortable existence, throwing us hard against the concrete of life. It is arbitrary, randomly secular and often feels unjust. Many of us when applying for jobs possess the necessary qualifications to handle the roles we are assigned. Therefore, every failed experience proudly displayed on a resume may simply highlight a mismatch or arise from a politically toxic environment. That is why I rarely rely solely on resumes to make my decisions in hiring. Resumes, like well-meaning mothers bragging to strangers about their extraordinary kids, are often untrustworthy and exaggerated. In interviews I study body language and how prepared they are for the job. I'll ask questions that are more specific to how they can handle pressure, setbacks and success. The other stuff, I can teach. As a manager, I prioritize understanding whether a candidate fits into the company culture.

For instance, when seeking an experienced sales rep for my Melbourne office, I received a resume and an impressive cover letter from a young lady with an almost flawless sales background. We spoke over the phone and then I interviewed her in person. She was intelligent, articulate, impeccably groomed and she answered my questions with precision as if she had foreseen them and prepared thoroughly. I had an instinctive apprehension. She seemed too perfect, perhaps even performative. She passed every standard interview test that was given to her. Her references were believable and full of praise. She stood out, no doubt, from the others I interviewed. I was prepared to hire her, but still I wasn't convinced. I decided to use my old unorthodox approach to interviewing by using the matrix of character hunting.

I called her and told her I'd be in town on a particular day and suggested we meet at a café at the end of the day to continue our talks. When we met something unexpected happened, which left me disturbed. Instead of ordering coffee she opted for a few glasses of wine. The wine loosened her up, and she flirtatiously told me "I will do anything to get the job". I finished my one drink, got up, paid the bill, wished her well and left. The next day I sent her an email informing her that she did not get the job. Within a few days she responded with a lengthy tirade about her exceptional abilities, arguing why she was perfect for the role and questioning her rejection. A few more emails followed. I chose not to respond to any of them. It's a good policy not to engage with someone unscrupulous. It generally leads to nowhere. From my perspective, she failed the most important test - the test of character.

CHAPTER 14

Two teams – one does all the work!

Why do you think talented sales reps migrate in great numbers to management like the many hopeful refugees crossing borders? Is it less bloody, more civilized and less accountable? To some degree, yes, it's a safer haven if you are one of the decision-makers in the corporate hierarchy. Behind the curtains are where decisions on tactics and strategy are constructed, that will decide a person's future within a company and the outcome of their career and reputation. It is a formidable place where the corporate gods gather and play to ponder and devise activities to build a company's fortune. Good managers will spend more time supporting their sales reps that need experience and trust by being on calls with them. Too many times, managers are in their offices staring at spread sheets or rationalizing numbers without understanding their true meaning. Management is a strange word for leading human productivity. What exactly are you managing? Time?

Resources? Growth? People? Your superior?   Managers should look at themselves as simply a natural extension of their sales reps. When a sales rep is promoted to management, they may distance themselves from the daily sales activity to join the ranks of the directors who need binoculars to get a clear view of client relationships and the positionality of engagement. Managers should be the public servants of the revenue generators.

One activity that is going on is "hiding the pea under the shell" game that managers love to play with everyone. A shuffle here, a shuffle there. It's the follow-the-pea street hustle game that is played, more to create a blurred vision than as strategic warfare. It's an art form all its own that leaves frontline teams wondering about reality and the real goals of the company. The shell game involves deception and hidden maneuvers. For example, a sales manager may reassign a client to another rep, and this happens often. The shuffling of clients may not be in the best interest of the business. I've seen this practice of giving a sales rep only three months to establish business from a client, under threat of losing the client and potential revenue. It's highly manipulative and mostly unproductive. In industries where relationships are paramount, rotating clients based on arbitrary time limits undermines the efforts of good sales reps and will negatively impact the client.

The pea inside the shell is the internal politics or the nepotism that is hard to see. The trick is the guess work, where the manager controls the decision and the movement, but surprisingly not the outcome. This lack of transparency behind the decisions creates distrust and confusion within the sales team when clients are shuffled randomly. All sales reps are affected and undervalued by lazy and deceptive management biases. This is not to say that some clients should not be moved. But before that happens, management needs to establish clear and transparent criteria by providing feedback and support about the progress with a client, to ensure that the sales rep is allowed enough time to improve. As a senior manager observing teams, I have seen too much shuffling based primarily on internal politics and nepotism, rarely on ability.

You have two teams in a business – the front-line staff: sales, marketing, administration and local sales managers, and the behind-the-curtain staff: senior directors, board members and investors. The two teams rarely meet up. Whichever team you're on, it may not feel like you're working for the same company.

Let's picture the boardroom as a modern-day court of emperors and priests, draped in titles far removed from the day-to-day execution of the company. We understand it is a meeting place for serious review, vision statements and often detached concerns. Collectively, they raise the flag of assessments and direction for the company. A rhetorical refuge of high-titled executives – some politically stacked, others pure gold – and likely the starting point for where the unbalance begins. Sitting with old world emperors, and their kneeling attendants and banker priests, I envision them looking down from a higher perspective at the chattering class of "doers". They are ever-present to serve the shareholders. The investors watch anxiously, read reports that are heavily filtered to accentuate their interest in money and more money. Collectively within their low literary IQ, they wouldn't know the difference between iceberg lettuce and the Antarctic. It may sound harsh, but the saturation of sameness and progenitors of genealogy-based-on-nepotism undoubtedly prevents a crafting of tailored solutions that constitute a holistic approach to balance and successful interactions.

Progress and innovation are sacrificed for short-term growth to enhance a playbook for investors or potential investors. The uptick of Cuban heels for men wouldn't have been invented if it weren't for petite gangsters and The Beatles, or if the board were stacked by tall Harvard graduates. Short guys aside, the market would have never noticed its growth if it weren't for a moment of marketing genius.

The board game – or room – is a majestic illusion of grandeur and rightful privilege with some good old-fashioned pretence. I am not saying the esteemed members are not sincere in their lofty goals of profit. Oh, they are! I am just addressing their status, rank and dress-up.

All the information that passes as a tribute to objectivity, true or false, is shared in concert. It is conspiratorial and studious within closed rooms of confidence, influence and lascivious power. There are enough adequate solutions, respectable debates and tossed about opinions, mixed with mental-blank fear, good-scout intentions, valuable experience and tired marketing garbage, that ultimately the sales reps are required to empty onto the agency's indifferent streets. Ideas will be conformed, shaped and cozied. The rehashed, rarely ever retooled, or original idea may never see the light of day. Unless the captain known as the CEO is tough and willful.

Although it is revered in some places in villages high above the Andes, the boardroom is not a mystical subterranean grotto with eccentric magicians floating on pearl shells chanting spells and incantations to deliver profits. There are no magical *formulae* or ancient ceremonial prayers. It is bland. It is sober. It is like having a dinner party with accountants, funeral directors, embalmers or your elderly mother's best friend.

It is a button-down place for button-down ideas. It is a simple-yet-complex meeting place with people chosen of different compositions to tick a diversity and inclusion checkbox. Seldom does that ever happen. It is as exciting as talking about music to the tone deaf or your elderly mother's best friend.

The members of this elite group are not entirely devising, but more precise than that, they can always draw from the deep well of toads, unicorns and magicians. If ever they need an occasional fiery witch or wizard to lift the plasticine lid, they may possibly invite the latest can-do marketing director or soft-mouthed golden retriever operations manager for a show-and-tell, or simply to pet. They spin magical spells, lap and bounce, mouthing mumbo-jumbo about spreadsheets, while chasing quacking ducks around the table of the anointed. Mostly, it's tedious.

On the other hand, the front-line staff are the lifeblood of any business. I've never heard of a business imploding because of good sales results. The sales reps are the catalysts for generating revenue. Their roles encompass prospect identification and laying the groundwork for future sales and relationships. They negotiate rates by discussing pricing, ensuring the company remains profitable. They closely collaborate with clients, crafting strategies and fostering a sense of partnership. Many times, they operate in an unpredictable and often volatile market, requiring their sales reps to be agile and adaptable to different strategies. They must also trust that their support teams are not only competent, but that they are aligned with client expectations. They champion their product when they intimately understand the strengths and weaknesses of their product. The front-liners have a demanding role that requires determination, dedication and a passion to excel.

CHAPTER 15

Nice genitals.

To have an employee/employer love affair is a nasty, corrupt business activity and should not be engaged in, whether you are the higher or lower ranked within the business. The office is not an online dating service unless you work for eHarmony.

There are those of us who target a specific person based solely on the appearance of power and influence within their coveting hearts; while others, their runaway desire is to become in some way fixed to the company brand, the company culture and the managers genitals or, nicely put, pudendum— in fact the whole caboose is exposed! If you put out deliberately for your supervisor, you are either immorally ambitious or Machiavellian extreme. I'm not talking about an alcohol-induced, blanks-in-the-brain lustful opportunity. This "party of two" is happening Monday to Friday on a normal workday. Managers screwing staff in a nasty power grab fest, is more common in the office than a 10 a.m. coffee break—all behind closed doors.

I never understood how, in the light of day, an employer and employee can transition from studying spreadsheets to being spreadeagled on the desk.

This type of conduct reveals a deep, unsettling exploitation of power, influence and favors. It undermines the company's trust and respect to the others in the workplace. It creates a toxic environment for all employees. It tarnishes the overall integrity of the organization. If the company you work for does not have a zero-tolerance stance on this reprehensible behaviour, I suggest you leave the company before you become jaded or manipulated as well. Don't throw away your career... or your morals.

Many times, all over this ass-kissing world, I have seen the "I have arrived" sales reps tasked as porter, driver, babysitter, concierge, shopper, maid and butler, closet umbrella and ego masseuse for a rapturous and openly pleased employer and his family. The boss has a wife (or husband) who often is incapable of using the phone to request an Uber. Therefore, an energetic employee is assigned to be her driver and handle any additional tasks she may have. This employee feels blessed that she or he is chosen. This employee becomes part of a fabricated "family" created by the boss and their spouse, enjoying privileges and advantages over peers. The boss uses this divisive strategy to sow seeds of conflict and fear among employees. It's a cunning tactic to distract staff and undermine cohesion. Through superficial charm and insincere relationships, employees are burdened with invisible obligations, fostering deceit and building a network of informants to report any deviation from the company's questionable values. Such weak management tactics are unacceptable and should never be tolerated in any workplace. Those who willingly become part of this "family" should also be removed to restore a performance-based meritocratic environment. Unfortunately, they are often promoted to very senior positions way above their experience or potential

I worked with several sales reps in South America who were excited to have the company's logo tattooed conspicuously on their arm. These were straight-up-and-down people. They did not take drugs, at least regularly, and they were not geeky comic art fans. Their expression of love for their company was pious and dutiful, like Catholics taking communion in a Brazilian gilded church.

My first reaction when I heard about this inscription was disbelief, or that my translator was just having fun with my inability to learn the local language. When I saw her raised eyebrow expression, I knew something was not right in South America. Then I found out that their delightful manager was even more aghast at this permanent proposition.

One sales rep with limited English skills rolled up his sleeve to expose the back of his arm to point to where this permanent mark was to be inked. I was at a loss for words (at least in Portuguese) and at the same time disheartened. My quick-tongued translator could not find the accurate words in her brain word search to express this fast collision with loony during this unreal moment. I felt sad for his simpleness, his genuineness and his misplacement of loyalty. He wasn't doing it to have the company notice him. He was simply proud of working for this appreciative company.

What I felt he needed was a good dose of employee skepticism to build independence as its shepherd, rather than the blind faith to a political party membership, with a tattoo logo of a company that one day will have little use for him. The heavy consequence of too many of-the-moment promises will eventually rupture his confidence and trust. The tattoo will look stupid, even if bad things never happen.

Perhaps his meaning in the context of life and job was far too great, too deep and too devotional. In places like Brazil, you hang on to your job like a devout Catholic clutching a blessed rosary. That tattoo may have added purpose by attaching his identity to a group that would have not been as strong outside the daily office activity and paycheck. Whatever the underlying reasons, it was a bad decision. I knew his intention was earnest and not necessarily dumb, but I also knew he needed to interpret his loyalty in a more positive and less permanently *marked* way. Like demonstrating the attributes of excellence in his work. In this case, listen to his manager.

There are the breathless, tired souls that wander like displaced nomads from job to job, looking for a special warm place that will offer solace, fairness and family. Their copycat resumes are everywhere, scattered like cheap ideas in bland, disinterested offices.

I did advise him, with my insufferable way of mixing uncomfortable sarcasm with truth. I simply told him to instead consider a pot smoking skull or his pet dog as a tattoo. I learned later he is superstitious of skulls, and he never liked his dog.

My suggestion or comment as a humorous image did not cross over well in translation with my now-brain-fried translator. Her twisted face expelling nonsensical words made the moment even more spectacularly surreal when she confused the pot smoking part as an offense that could send him to prison and proceeded to give him a stern lecture on the evil of doing drugs and being responsible.

While my translator and my sales rep were shouting, in a highly agitated Brazilian state, wildly and animatedly arguing about pot, politics and pets, I drifted to the back of my mind and thought about disappearing ink as a solution to remaining a drifter manager or just disappearing.

And then as my mind traveled on the Grateful Dead highway, I thought how strange it would be if by some cosmic coincidence the disappearing tattoo and his job faded into oblivion at precisely the exact moment. What if he doesn't continue to make the constantly elevated grade his company expects, or if he were a female and happened to be an attractive woman and the boss's wife couldn't handle her husband working with her? I finished my third *cachaça* and headed back to my hotel, alone. Scratching my thoughts like a bearded cat reading beat poetry in a litter box.

This is what truly happened. Although, I wished it were only my imagination, flying from desk to desk like an upside-down cockroach about to be squashed, dreaming of invincibility. As far as I know he never got the tattoo. I saw him hug the translator and they made up with air kisses, love and laughter. I love Brazil.

If an infatuation for your employer is that overly obsessive and you need to express devotional love with a brand tattoo, why not first try to practice the intricate art of selling and then sell more and sell well, forever? If you don't have the inclination or the energy for ongoing success, have a long, second look at that Cartier watch you've been daydreaming about and perhaps think about trading it in for a grinning, affable and reliable Timex. One way or another—you are toast! Unless you rise above the consequences of desire and infatuation.

Always remember this, as you swing athletically across the monkey rings: you are not a sheet of metal in a factory, to be stamped and fitted. You are a human being that has provided a great service in supporting the growth and livelihood of all involved, from internal and external sources. This is not a joking matter when you must shape your behavior and align your "self" to a colorless company, run by colorless accountants and lawyers. Pay attention first to you, the person.

As a sales rep, even those with a self-given grandiose title, there is that invisible line you will cross when you are slapped with a surprise moment in your life that alters your nature. You will stand up and learn it is solely the revenue that endears your boss to you, even if your boss is fair and benign. It is not necessarily you, and achieving and exceeding budgets is the only "blanket" that will keep you safe, secure and warm—a blanket of discipline and learning that should be knitted into your professional tapestry. There is nothing cold about having to bring in revenue. It is fittingly expected, and it is the career you signed up for.

And for those that insist on tattooing their company's logo, either positioning it in full view on your arm or discreetly on your confused ass? Well, congratulations, you have just taken your first step into an alternative reality without booze or drugs. Something gonzo journalist Hunter S. Thompson never did sober. He'd be proud!

CHAPTER 16

Everything is negotiable.

You need strong negotiation skills to leverage good and bad relationships and preserve the company you work for, allowing for growth and expansion. If you simply go out into the market evolving as a derivative in boldness, you will place your income and the company's credibility at risk with your awkwardness and stilted business language.

Negotiation is a skill that will come in handy in every aspect of your life, be it personal or business. Despite all the toughness I see in the streets of Sydney or New York, I have found that many businesses are defined by a culture of friendship. Not that friendship isn't important; it is the basis for establishing trust and familiarity. But it is in negotiation where that friendship can break down.

The relationship can become more important to the seller or the buyer than the fairness of the deal. The familiarity from the buyer's side will insidiously create complacency, and they may think that just going to lunch or taking a walk in the park, will suffice to complete the transaction.

The untrained in serious negotiations are more common than the flu. Instead, potentially great sales reps have become loose and proficient in the discounting void. It's quick and easy. It's expedient to give the client exactly what they want by devaluing the product and quickly padding your commissions.

The seller calls it "closing the deal"; the client and their agents and the industry will call it "added value". I have witnessed this artless concession of discounting as it continues to be invited by both senior and junior media sales reps – and signed off by anxious managers –before any negotiations are even placed on the table. That is if negotiations are allowed these days.

The greatest con from buyers is "I don't have time to negotiate; I need an answer now". It has something to do with a sharp pencil or a keyboard as the new rule in arbitration. Everyone is busy with the "no time for this or that" syndrome.

At the beginning and end of all discussions during your negotiations, product performance and its uniqueness and value should be the main topic. By providing clients "value" within the sphere of a total-product experience, you can often eliminate the need to cut the price. You can also highlight your product's benefits with market intel, research *pseudo-science* and competitive knowledge. This will supersede any token gifts like company water bottles, phone chargers and muffins that you might think you need.

Some discerning clients pretend to be thankful for the corporate gifts you might give them, but they truly seek genuine product benefits and real experiences, not just the empty words of a sales rep. Once the tempting incentives such as bonuses, discounts, extravagant getaways or lavish parties are stripped away, your product will face the real test. You may soon realize that these freebies were not heralds of loyalty, but merely incentives to those who are bombarded daily with an abundance of offers. Focus on negotiating to persuade, rather than seducing with extras. Sell the product, not the add-ons. If you must, add value to the client's purchase, related to the core product. Perhaps you have another small product that might also suit them and add value to their experience with your core product? Offer that at a discounted rate for their first purchase, to allow them to try it out. That way, you may just increase the number of products that they buy from you going forward, and they might be similarly happy that you have filled a gap they didn't know they have. Now you are really becoming an advisor to their business – a valuable business partner.

Make discounts the last resort in the negotiating process.

I've watched sales reps who never truly sold the product. They sold the discount, but not the product. Your supersonic influence was an illusion, concocted by a tactic that diverts from the client's eye of appraisal understanding the true value of your product.

You may be a fun and generous rep to hang out with – many get hired for their lively personality and toothy grin – but I can guarantee you whenever you "drop your undies", you drop your credibility and integrity by exposing a desperate attempt to win business. My question remains to all clients, are there other clients who are getting more benefaction? A resounding "yes" is the answer. You might as well take their undies to the cleaners.

In time your good deeds will go unnoticed, and your client will want more fun things. They'll eventually go to your competitor to see what goodies they have in their pantry. The business of sales is never satiated; it is the business of wanting more. The sleight-of-hand practice of disappearing inventory, word trickery, discounting and mutual intimidation is nothing but fear-selling. The fear is real enough, agreed. It is at times heavy handed. The market, and you and your competitors, exploit it every day.

Products that are commoditized by unimaginative, aggressive advertising agencies are everywhere. And greedy, short-sighted sales managers have a confident belief that the better deal is in the discount, not the products' features and benefits. Convincing them is another story all together. Uh, it requires selling!

The nuances of what is done and how to get a sale over the line are as varied as the different dialects in many countries and geographical areas. There is no precise language in commerce. Tiny lies and bigger exaggerations are commonly accepted, overlooked and rehearsed. Therefore, it is not considered unethical or an untruth. It's ceremoniously backed up with research, advertising messages, fake news, over the top personality sales reps and promotional hyperbole. A splintering of language and a large community of interpretation in a multicultural business community.

While working in the United States, I negotiated a TV-media schedule with a well-established national advertising agency. They represented many blue-chip clients. This client was a major Eastern Seaboard supermarket chain.

According to the rather godless lady I was negotiating with, her primary demographic was women between 18 and 24 years of age. I was suspicious that she may have invented a false demographic to force me to drop our rates. At that time, I represented a sagging CBS affiliate with an older demographic.

I know that women are counted as the highest proportion of customers, but at that life stage their influence in grocery spending reaches as far as asking their mom to teach them how to prepare poached eggs on toast for their nondescript boyfriends.

The *lip-gloss* demo by this agency hustler really needed to consider expanding her demographic to include a wider field of age and lifestyles: singles, married, gay, children, no children and, of course, how about some average men. She also needed a conscience or to consider possible future employment as a loan shark. She used opportunistic macro-level ageism combined with a make-believe demographic to achieve her goals and sought-after rate. Her tactic to achieve her rate was played without regard to ethics or fairness. She cleverly showcased a narrow demographic to reach her desired outcome by manipulation and deceit. To allow her to get the juiciest deal from a television network whose prime audience was considered in the old folk's category of adults over 35 years of age.

This unashamedly confrontational agency buyer (okay, there was some admiration on my part) with the mouth of an entire drunken football team on a losing night out, finally agreed that she would burn in hell for this. I calmly, but with my voice shaking said, "If the primary demo in supermarkets is in fact women between the ages of 18-24, wouldn't supermarkets be the number one social hub and pick-up joint for guys?". She growled some more expletives. Her response showed not just aggression, but perhaps the frustration at being challenged.

A quick thought came to me during the expletive negotiation, that is, if grocery shopping is an arousal activity, then there is nothing sexier than a shopping cart stuffed with ripe bananas, low fat milk, and Honey Nut Cheerios, sitting messed up in a metal or plastic container being pushed or carried by a Friday night *hoochie-mama* at Aldi. I didn't share this thought with her. Her hostile demeanor was escalating.

If I continued to play along with her fantasy demo to meet her goal, I would have to heavily cut my rates or bake the most unrealistic rate "cake" possible, layered with a cream of bonuses, and provide her and her schnoodle with a cottage in Provence. I did nothing. I suggested that we re-negotiate her demographic first, bringing it more in line with their real customers. Or I walk. I knew she wouldn't let me walk because of the amount of time she had spent on the phone with me and her lather of swearing. She agreed to redefine her perimeters.

The hours of sweaty negotiations were surreal. At the end, surprisingly, we found a legitimate compromise. We agreed to a demo of women aged 18-54 as more reasonable. I was able to offer rate concessions for her flexibility without severely discounting it. I should have pushed for all people 18-54 years of age, but by then I was dealing with men issues, mother issues and all the other sucker stuff from her mouth that assaulted my brain. Besides it was late, and I wanted to go home. I'd had enough.

Admittedly, my share of the business shrunk proportionately after I exposed her gambit, but at the end I was able to sell the saved inventory to other advertisers at an equitable and profitable yield. It was a better outcome for the company, but not necessarily for my pocket.

There truly were no personal benefits for me, other than keeping aggressive negotiations away from the biggest share of our inventory, receiving a smaller slice. It kept my rate healthy, my boss happy and my bonus offer minimal. It helped our company's earnings as we continued to establish rate believability with this agency, their clients and the market.

I fought hard, yet fairly, to protect our rate and our products' reputation. Months later, my negotiations for the next round with this same person were respectful and her language semi-normal. My share just happened to increase without acquiescing to another pretend demographic, manufactured solely for a price advantage. The buyer knew we were both being thrown into a tough negotiation arena, but she respected me for at least meeting her part of the way and pushing back. A few months later she opened to me and said she was leaving the agency. According to her, they burned out talent, the stress was heavy, and her health was being compromised. The money was good, but it just wasn't worth her peace of mind. We remained business friends for many years after. As it turns out, she was really a lovely person when the extraordinary stress was removed.

I repeat – and it's worth repeating – there are sales reps who choose not to sell their product; they sell the discount. They represent a result much closer to their personal earnings, and their personal friendships, which is inimical from the sales goals of maximizing value or the company's interest.

They will gush and affirm over and over about their self-claimed unique client friendship that is irreplaceable. Especially the mystical power they wield over them. They are the masters of self-overestimation and hubris. You will hear them boasting loudly from a manager's office "No other sales rep can manage this client as well as I do". They will add with pride and reinforcement "this agency won't deal with anyone but me". Or the same reverberation from a sometime manager, who shadows sales reps for their personal benefit and fresh air. It's an agreeable atmosphere for self-love. It's a plea from a diminished business that has been forecast to grow. To keep the charade alive and turning. The friendship is always questionable; people tend to be self-motivated. The rates are stagnant, perhaps reversing. Bonuses are a given and always inclusive. Lunches are frequent and personal. It happens a lot and it is a pattern. This is when a sales rep places too much authority on their "faithful loving relationship" with the buyer. One day it just happens—they stop selling. They stop doing good business. They continue offering gifts and promoting their client love affair to naïve managers and themselves. They flourish in their misrepresentation. They are compensated handsomely by the company to only maintain the status quo and block growth for a few air kisses.

If you push your own agenda, whatever unrealistic form it takes, be advised you are pushing business out the door. The chances of a discounting or friendship crutch will unfortunately force you and the company to lose profits and become more commoditized and less valuable. You will be forced to do the awkward back movement of a limbo competition: how low can you go? Forced to layer obese and careless concessions to the point where you don't have the luxury to discern a distinction, a difference and your product's true value.

Commission sales reps become hazardous waste if they are fiddling with the fiddler's fiddle. Commissions should be rewarded, yes, but skewed not just on the sale – that is routinely graded towards a personal budget accomplished or not – but on a higher level of price points, to deliver a consistently greater value for a premium and its boastful disparity. It's called real share of business. Many companies are losing tens of thousands, to millions, of dollars each by blindly accepting any exchange called activity or promise.

This is unlikely to change if managers continue to accept poorly constructed business thinking to feed the salivating, uncaged, jaundiced-eyed monkey who is ready to strike. Company budgets are then in fast moving sunshine clouds created by CFOs and CEOs to please banks and shareholders and their bulging bank accounts. These overpaid, oversized titles analyze the data of the dead – like trusting a gangster family to safeguard your fortunes against illegitimate benefactors or unworthy relatives.

Alas, we are left with corporate rowdiness, head-shaking buffoonery and grinning monkeys, picking each other's fleas and pointing long or short fingers. These silver backs become experts at finding blame, firing staff and acting like aggrieved debutantes with a broken heel.

The budget is rolled out and fixed with superglue unless there is a pandemic or a wholesale change of staff. In the meantime, both managers and reps are apprehensive and excitable. The creaky carousel goes "round and round" finger pressed hard on the big red button by a sluggish seasonal roustabout. And discounting remains as normal as cheese and toast in a microwave.

It is always wise to know your product intimately and return to it often and learn about it again as time goes on. This will give you the courage, the confident and unruffled certainty, and the psychological advantage that comes from knowing that your product is of value to the client. It will stop you from offering too many incentives, blessings and concessions in your negotiations. You will be challenged but must remain calm and confident. You can negotiate. Your product is good; it will be good for the client. It will help them.

Before you go into any meeting, you should have responses to all probable objections prepared and ready to be addressed. This is critical to enable affinity in negotiations. I worked for a global company, and in my experience the objections were identical, whether I was in Brazil, Japan or

Muskogee, USA. It was easy to handle objections in any language or mind set.

Your argument must then correlate with the objection, not with fear of the unknown or ignorance. Do not quickly counter the objection (usually it is price) by dismissing it or telling the client they are wrong.

Listen carefully to the objection and discuss the matters in depth, convincingly, so the client feels comfortable and open to your argument. Leverage empathy, past and current results and sincerity to establish trust—by being in accord with their concerns. You are not an intruder.

If it's about price you won't have to reduce yourself as a cheap transactional rep. You have a better grasp of what is really at the heart of it. Find the fit first; answer it clearly and persuasively. Keep the conversation away from price and steer it towards the value of the product if you're sitting at the table.

Your asking price will generally be accepted if you learn client-centric habits like active listening. It's the only way to successfully forge a real and lasting relationship with the client and their business. If you do not ask relevant questions, and you have a limited understanding of who and what they represent, then you are an intruder or worse, a bagman. The future is but one question away.

CHAPTER 17

The multifaceted nature of identity and the never-ending job interview.

We draw conclusions and base opinions on what we see in an instant. Memory is insolvent (metaphorically speaking). We draw portraits of ourselves from remnants of the past. The highlights of pride and achievement or a dark traumatic event, like a divorce or illness, become magnified in the presence of love, pain or regret. Who we are to family, friends and strangers can be a permanent impression or a jarring impulse. Believability is the construct contained in our mind and body as we travel each day from familiar to unfamiliar and then repeat. Inside, this acquisition of knowledge in various sacred and unholy sacrifices, is synthesized. It is joined together from our experiences of books we've read, from our teachers, past lovers and mentors, then blending with the debilitating fear and surprising bravery that visit us from time to time in our consciousness, like a lost family reunited.

A Native American poet once said something that struck a chord with me. I don't recall his name or where I heard it, but here it is. He was quoted as saying "we look at all sides of the person from the front, back, left and right—to see who they really are." This multi-perspective gazing, seeing all sides, will give you a profound understanding of other's opinions and arguments, whether in difficult sales negotiations or casual discussions. The chance of a winning conclusion or breakthrough increases and people become more interesting. So do you. It's the concept of judging a book by its cover. To know the book (the client) you must read it. When the Native American says he looks at all sides, he is saying he has read the book. In sales you must look at all sides of an argument – and of a person – to craft a meaningful narrative.

To change one's mind is an act of intelligence; it is not skittish meandering. Understandably there are those who are glued to their opinion. To have a mind shift can be as difficult as moving to Egypt wearing a pink kilt. The transoceanic pounding of uncontrollable waves overriding all familiar associations and attachments, beating at your learned concrete beliefs and values, testing your adaptability and empathy to unpredictable currents. In sales you must have mind agility.

Perhaps to go further or deeper would be going too far, with too much serious thinking and effort. To ask thoughtful questions may reveal too much of what we need to know. And who needs honesty, right? Even more to the point, who needs to work harder if you can get away with less? Some books preach that in a minute you can do almost anything. If you're a reader of business books you may read "The One Minute Manager". Like instant, precooked Minute Rice, a popular cooking helper in America, for when you don't have enough time to eat. How about when someone is speaking to you, and you tell them you only have a minute? When you want it that quick because of a fabrication of time, or poor time management, leaving no time to eat or even sell, you're skating on thin ice. Skating the surface, and hope for what is equal to the best, is an inferior method for doing anything of superior value, whether it's fast food or hype-selling.

We judge people with a glance or a categorized opinion we picked up in social media, solely or with a like-minded group. Judging a book by its cover in sales is unreliable and tediously passive. Besides it's more rewarding to read the book.

In a job interview it seems the standard business of "getting to know you" is established by far-reaching questions.

The reality is, we never receive the actual "knowing them" truth of an accurate composition just looking indifferently – or one-sided – at an individual. Our life-learned biases are ever present, firmly entrenched in our minds. Professional interviewers will stare at you to see if you flinch, to test your psyche and to ultimately learn your true identity.

The judo-trained interviewer moves with dexterity through your resume with 20/20 vision, guiding themselves to a sharper presumption and harder fall. We are parlaying with nearsighted administrators trained for the generic roll call of the faceless, dressed in plain colors, extending a foot instead of a hand. Only one person ends up landing on their ass, and guess who?

Quite a few companies have a manual of questions to follow the "eye exam" from another untrained ophthalmologist with the vision of an earth worm. "Where do you see yourself in 5 years?" or "If you were a Chihuahua on a skateboard, how long would it take you to skate around the block without barking or showing teeth?", it goes on and on. Meanwhile your brain is desperately trying to understand this Greek, piecemeal game of *synecdoche*.

In a job interview in Kansas City, I was asked by a potential employer where I saw myself in 5 years. Clearly, I thought to myself, not in that job. I blurted out the words, like an unexpected loud fart on a first date, "hoping to never have to answer that question again". I got a chuckle but, not unexpectedly, the job.

Admittedly these self-described "serious companies" will add the big artillery with heavy-handed psychological tactics: the aim of getting a confession out of you with the torture of follow-up interviews from another chin-stroking interrogator.

The optimistic resume and beaten prisoner are further examined, and studied just to be sure, then moved up another line to an interview with more propaganda from a prescient human relations *bonobo* who, a minute ago, happily pressed a "like" icon on LinkedIn. To undoubtedly identify favorably with another "golly gee" comment or thumbs up.

The confused, skinny "prisoner" interviewee sits nervously, socks slowly dropping, and is working achingly hard inside to control their breathing and smile, by saying the wrong things and one big intimate fuck up!

Congratulations! After all that, the contest is finally between you and one other exhausted candidate for that seasonal job as a ride operator at Fantasy Fun Land. In the sales "carnival" we are subject to similar drawn-out mistakes, like those that interviewers make when they size people up for recreation.

Landing the perfect job when facing a difficult interviewer doesn't have a guaranteed formula. However, remaining genuine and positive is key. Avoid bagging your current boss or company, even if they deserve it. Instead provide influential references that will present an all-sides reflection of you and your abilities. Make sure your references are well prepared. I've encountered references who were critical and advised against hiring the candidate, which is awkward! To prevent this, contact your reference givers beforehand to discuss the position for which you're applying. Never assume that everyone loves you. Interviewing is a language managers must learn to accomplish, by bringing the best on board, and communicating to all in the company how high their standards are.

CHAPTER 18

Role-playing - everyone hates it!

There is one training technique that is loathed by all grades of sales reps. It is brutal in the minds of sales reps. It exposes the ability – or inability – to think on your feet and shape an argument. It can paralyse or mobilise you. It invites both criticism and praise, like an ugly baby or a church sermon. This ugly baby is called role-playing. Role-playing in a sales meeting as a training tool should be part and parcel of a sales executive's life. Well, fundamentally it should be, but it's not in most sales organisations. Managers would be money-wise to replace the standard dead-end sales meetings of "probe and defend" with "awareness and stimulation". Role-playing, if done right, should be mandatory for all sales reps regardless of rank. Does it really matter how many years in sales you have clocked up or how financially successful you are? Training and learning are the currency of continued success for life.

There are senior sales executives who are naturally self-conscious and carry in their persons a deep insecurity. The "I am a fake" mind talk. They will never express or lay open their proficient sales dialogue in the presence of colleagues, as they are unsure of themselves. It takes bravery and poise to deliver an unrehearsed exchange in front of management and peers.

Why is there such fear and push-back on something that will help you make more money or become more articulate with regards to your product and the market? Unfortunately, many senior sales reps believe their standing within the company will be compromised, or falsely graded, within a practice setting that does not represent their accomplishments or their true grit, when one on one with a client. To them it is only the juniors who need all the help that is offered. They need to be reminded that knowledge-from-experience is an examination for everyone who participates, no matter what grade. It will toughen up, and integrate with, your mental potential by merging the real and artificial in creating storytellers.

Role-playing is not a real-life situation, but it brings real gravity to your expression. It is mental *jiu-jitsu* to keep you fresh and agile in the meeting "dojo". It is far better to accept the uncomfortable in your workplace, with your uncomfortable peers who happen to feel the same way you do (with the same consequences) than it is to make costly mistakes on the street. If the rules of role-play are not stiff or intimidating, it's a fun environment, where your colleagues will be earnest and supportive. The benefit and discipline of role-play will bring with it greater product certainty and warm confidence when you are in a real-life setting.

Preparing for face-to-face interactions fosters maturity and confidence when presenting to buyers. Group alignment helps identify gaps in our arguments, while role-playing offers fresh, dynamic interpretations. Peers provide feedback using different perspectives, illuminating details that might have been overlooked.

There is no doubt that role-play exposes weak arguments and delivery. Personally, I have learned new ways of seeing my product many times over, even from entry level sales reps. They introduce outside eyes, fresh perspectives.

If you refuse to role-play, it is usually fear based and spiritless—frozen in the tyranny of your mind. Avoidance self-talk has nothing to do with talent or capacity, but everything to do with fear of peer judgement or of being exposed for not being up to date with your product.

But think about this—if you and your peers role-play often, you *will* be up to date.

Avoidance self-talk prevents engagement within the possibility of energizing innovative ideas. Undeniably this is where the real expansion-of-self happens – to the individual and, incidentally, the company's profits. A regular dose of role-play will not change your personality or lower your blood pressure, but it will assist in developing a grounded and genuinely persuasive argument. It will shape your argument as active, not passive, convincing not scripted.

Role-playing is animate, designed to encourage sharper accuracy, wider thinking, instant courage and the ability to think on your feet under pressure. One of the reasons to work and develop an unrehearsed situation is so that you know that you really do know your product.

This structure of learning will develop a sense of urgency and necessity followed by expansion and growth, knowing that what is taking place is immediate and timely. If your sales organization does not have a role-play component in your sales meetings, you should demand it, not only for what you may learn but also for a real collaboration with your peers and manager.

Role-playing is for all stages of your sales career. It is not just showing the novice how to untangle blistery ropes; it is for each and all to learn product articulation that is not forced or rehearsed. It is an exquisite and convincing preparation for the untamed streets.

Roleplay is not Sales 101 as one unhappy manager jeered; it is free climbing, and a raw, rugged mental exercise that strengthens your resolve. It is also intrinsically brave and fabulously unpredictable. It is physical, and it sets the tone within the framework of your communication composition to the marketplace.

Your peers will be helpful in comparing arguments with regards to the clarity and cohesiveness of your pitch, technique and language. Eventually the narrow, rougher edges are unjammed and your confidence and depth of knowledge will exceed expectations. The outcome of friendship and trust with your teammates will be one of many dividends offered to you.

It's a tool for mastering authentic and spontaneous product articulation – essential preparation for real-world challenges and, if properly executed, is akin to being irreverent, audacious, imperfect and inclusive. It should also be boisterous and animated. In other words, *fun*. Having shared ideas and group passion are the lifeblood of a healthy sales team. The workplace will be transformed as the breakthrough environment, giving force to your professional intellect without any fear of rejection or judgement. Role-play should never be considered punishment. It is not an excuse for harsh criticism, dogmatic projection or an oblique opening towards implementation of a rigid policy on performance if deemed unsuccessful, as some spreadsheet-focused managers might think. Involve them in the role-play session. Their participation transcends mere oversight or routine meetings, instead fostering collaboration and creativity.

Ultimately you will change your inner- and outer-self when you discover it yourself, as The Beatles once sang, "...with a little help from my friends".

CHAPTER 19

Ass kissing will give you hiccups.

A well-entrenched, follow-the-rules employee will become emotionally and ethically tied to the character and values of their employer, or perhaps one person at the top.

When you are picked to join the workforce of a company, you are relegated to strictly conform to their idiosyncrasies, which may remove the important parts of you and your identity. I am not talking about a choice of clothing, symbolic tattoos or the odd hardware on your face. The identity-fit that is critical to your professional success and disposition in the workplace is something remarkably unseen, bubbling inside. The values that accompany you to work are challenged, shifted and buried deep, then arise perhaps when money feeds the fire of your soul like dry kindle or anxious lust.

The culture that a company adopts isn't always contained within their mission statement hanging on a wall or hiding clumsily inside a desk. The culture, good or bad, slowly evolves, depending on its successes or failures and the hiring of individuals who place merit on their personal ambitions. This could be a young upstart quietly politicizing an overthrow, or a middle manager whose interest is in maintaining the status quo, that determine direction as a proxy from someone above. As employees we adjust and reposition ourselves, front and center, to be noticed or at least recognizable. Our desire for approval cannot be easily explained, however in the business world it is simple and cannot be ignored: power, money, esteem and control. Nothing else matters beyond the means to an end. The unforgiving manager who drives up budgets to impress his superiors knowing that it will be difficult to achieve but pushing for a result, one that manufactures insecurity and the displacement of good people. These one-eyed cyclops still push. An employee may see an opportunity to divert the pressure off themselves onto another. How often have you heard a colleague ask questions about, and ruthlessly evaluate, people by labeling them as small, medium and large in terms of influence? Influence can be fleeting, after all. You need to understand the workplace dynamics, and how you and everyone else fit into them, if you are to have some success in the organization. It's political and it's based wholly outside your assigned role and responsibilities. It's not what they teach in business schools. It's the "school of human foibles" that is overlooked as nothing to be concerned about—until it becomes concerning.

The politics of working within organizations is the community of humans who publicly seem likeable and agreeable. If you're unlucky, you'll learn that some people harbor grudges, misrepresent others, form tribal alliances, seek support and basically lick the ass of anyone they believe will accelerate them to another level. As Aristotle said, "we are mortal animals, despite our aspiration to be god-like".

We are caught in the natural web of necessity that makes us dependent on a particular environment. In between all this exhausting mental and emotional heavy lifting, we do find time for actual work. Work is intertwined with our character, ethics and ambitions. We surprise ourselves when we take a direction that is counter to the ethics and community politics within the company. We either leave the company or are removed. It is difficult to flourish outside the norms of collective interests. We rule and we are ruled over but to what end?

There are many different characters who chose a *schtick* to gain a pontifical blessing from their boss. One that is annoyingly nervy, is the "office licker". At first glance lickers are innocuous and may seem harmless. These are the folks with a hearty laugh, always ready to laugh at anything the supposedly clever boss says during his walk down the office corridor. While they might blend in, they often make it clear who they want to groom for favor. The boss confidently saunters into the sales pit with a delicious smile and talks about his new puppy and how it peed in his wife's new shoes. The boss says "I never liked those shoes. I guess Rolo didn't like them either". He chuckles repeatedly (a cue for everyone in the room to laugh). Then a roar of laughter from the licker, edging closer to lick his spotless runners.

Think about how many times bad jokes or ironic references have made you feel compelled to laugh or, at least, put on a fake smile. A sign of conformity planted on your mouth like a plastic butterfly with stretched wings. Welcome to the political world of corporate ass-kissing. Okay, some would say that it is not necessarily ass-kissing, but more a show of respect or just being polite. Perhaps it's just a bad case of the hiccups in the form of laughter. Once it starts it can feel like it lasts an eternity and it's annoying.

The superego deputizes the powerless! It begins to control with bad humor. It controls our good judgement. It forms opinions based on how well you conform, bow and behave. The real or authentic *self* is buried deep like dead relatives you met occasionally when they were alive. This is the bargain: A good income and job security in exchange for dad jokes and a magical corporate life filled with approval on the snakes and traps trail. The office's game of "cat and mouse" offers insights into managing your professional life. You have a choice: Engage in petty attacks on individuals or adopt the role of a mysterious lone wolf. The lone wolf route may seem easiest but make sure you don't become a target to the rest of the staff. Focusing solely on your work rather than being distracted by office personalities is generally good for you and the business you work for. Just keep in with the other staff members, as well as the boss.

Which leads me to another dangerous position to uphold. If your boss uses you as an information-on-the-ground source, pressing you to reveal inappropriate details about other staff members, they may not be happy. This might be misconstrued as a promotion to "confidant" and therefore pits you against them.

The key is balance. The balance of your work friendships against your engagement with superiors.

Ultimately while office politics can't be entirely avoided, focusing on balancing a professional life will provide fulfillment. The cycle of office politics can be disruptive, often causing changes in who holds influence. I've observed many times how the dynamic shifts, replacing one player with another. It's common for some employees to spend excessive time in the boss's office, currying favor and advancing personal agendas. However, focusing on developing innovative ideas and building strong work habits will naturally lead to success, without the need for political maneuvering.

Some may believe you need to be politically savvy, adopting strategies purely for survival for fear that others might undermine you. Yet, there is another art to survival and growth without destructive political engagement. This involves becoming well acquainted with your industry, proficient in market trends and maintaining a strong, unwavering network of client relationships. True power lies in avoiding behaviors that compromise your professionalism and self-worth. Many books have been written about office politics and how to thrive in a hostile environment. Read them and learn the art of survival (not war) in a positive way, to present your nature as "straight". To paraphrase Marcus Aurelius, "It is better to be straight than to be straightened". Wise words and great advice. I've seen many people in my travels who accomplished the art and study of their profession without spilling any blood. You must invest in yourself and be brave.

"Nothing is more natural than for the cat to love the rat"
– Zin-Yang Kuo, Chinese scientific philosopher

CHAPTER 20

Courage!

In the world of business, courage is both a beacon of success and a disruptor of the status quo. Its bold defiance inspires, but it can also isolate, challenging conformity and unsettling the comfortable norms around it. Courage is learned and practiced; the development of courage will build more strength with insight and change within. Courage is saying and doing the right thing unfailingly—it is not always about being right. It is more about ethics and values, never about perfection. Courage is staying on your path regardless of temptation or a short cut. It is about action and reinforcing your integrity.

You can feel and hear the honor of courage mixing with your blood as it guides and strengthens your movement and word muscles. Its palpable presence can be seen in the eyes of others, from the complex gaze to the simple acceptance. Saying "no" is not offensive; it's often an act of courage. It sheds a bright light on boundaries by knowing that "maybes" are pointlessly dragging a "no" to the eventuality of a true response. In fact, it is the "DNA sibling" to curiosity, which provides answers and clarity. Courage is the connection to curiosity, bridging a broadened narrative by fueling exploration and trust. Courage is open to all possibilities. You will be the one to decide which of the two paths you will take in your life. One path straight—or one path crooked, bent by pleasing others or misguided underhandedness. Each decision you make, or allow others to make for you, will be the measure of your courage and your versatility in human engagement. People will listen and trust your guardianship if they hear steadfast, honest courageous words from you, and then watch you put it into action.

If you bend to an expectation that is compromised for a quick win or a sloppy solution, your validity and who you are will be diminished, and your product's validity and what it can deliver suspiciously challenged. Courage is the persistence of nature rather than an antidote to the fear of losing or falling behind. Fear is like the echo of your parents telling you repeatedly "No" as a child. It is self-limiting and it will prevent you from expanding and growing.

The consequence of fear is procrastination. Courage prepares you to avoid delaying difficult tasks that in time will add unnecessary pressure to completion and activity. With fear you will become as aimless as autumn leaves drifting in the wind. It is a departure from a solid foundation. Fear is your false partner in deceit and apathy.

Courage is a daily mental and physical workout; it's multifaceted. Courage is inimitable by underscoring its unique value. Always aim and prepare for the best, and you will build courage to connect all the harmonious parts that make you a consistently transparent person in your business and in your life. It is this transformation that becomes ingrained in you by developed, consistent effort. It's not easy to find and use your voice.

Fear on the other hand is the tedious and weak excuse that hides good intention and value. It supports the *status quo* and lowers the potential for growth and innovation. In business, it is considered the norm to exaggerate, to lie and use "pretzel logic" in negotiations with customers and co-workers. Set your sights higher and reach within for authenticity, even when faced with pressure to conform to lower and less-honest standards.

If you follow the advocacy of identity without compromise, you will speak to a broader audience – not overshadowed by personal interest – and emerge as the greater version of who you are. You will be sought after and respected as an authoritative resource. The ability to live like a true human, and earn an income equally as rewarding, is a difficult goal to achieve when you are asked to shift, manipulate or cheat.

Your work, or the esteemed title you wear, should not untie your true connection to yourself or those who pay your way.

An exemplary act of courage is standing up to your boss when it jeopardizes their integrity. I recall an incident where a manager instructed sales reps to disguise a product flaw by "fudging" the numbers – a term that might sound innocuous, but we all knew it implied unethical conduct. One sales rep, however, courageously refused to comply, recognizing it was a breach of her ethics and values. She voiced her concern to the manager in front of her fellow sales team members, who remained silent and passive, accepting the direction of management as gospel.

Her bold stance, although admired, led to strained relations with her manager. After that public exchange, he spent an inordinate amount of time finding fault with her work and her person. It ultimately led to her dismissal. This was a strong signal the manager sent to the sales team—obey or you're finished. She swiftly rebounded and secured a managerial role with a competitor. Her faith in her beliefs demonstrates how courage can lead to personal victories. A big win for courage and the industry.

Here is a poem of mine, titled "The Worker". I wrote this using metaphors and themes to critique societal expectations and conformity. At times we are forced or compelled to hide our true selves and thus present an expectation of ourselves to others. A lot of our interactions are guided by conformity and a fear that dominates our social structure and the rigidity of work. We're easily molded or fitted. Bravery advocates mindfulness. If you understand the nature of bravery, that each person has this trait within them, that it can be developed in relation to our work and personal life, true success will follow.

"THE WORKER"

The foundation of our lives and humanity,
inside an intrusive wireless family
Supporting our interactions,
in obedience, and awe.
The face mask isn't the horror,
the disingenuous grin behind the mask is.
The mask is tightly fitted and compact,
manufactured bought, sold, and resold.
A global franchise of human obedience,
from the young to the established old

An infinite assembly line of easily removable parts,
attached to broken dreams and broken hearts.
The face mask protects all complicit possibilities.
Be careful which one you wear.

CHAPTER 21

The imposter syndrome.

Consider this a hard slap to the face from a quite common and overly exploited adage we have heard countless times from clueless managers during the span of our sales careers: "You are only as good as your last order". Is this tenet based on averages or real numbers at last count? Or literally, your last order? Is it a metaphor for the crime of falling out of favor? Is it a hidden, secret code based on privilege or a long list of primordial backbiting? Is it based on advantage? Is it based on simply being a shit sales rep packing a heavy dose of reality? There is one thing we do know and that is what keeps sales reps up at night—the fear of obsolescence. The fear of falling behind. The fear of never writing another order. And the fear of losing those air-kissing work friendships that will instantly disappear.

In my experience the bottom line is the only line on the fact sheet that is sober and used to measure performance of the company and people. Those numbers, like a good referee, decide the points in making or not making budgets. The score sheet determines your value and reputation. As with Moses and his Ten Commandments, this is sacrosanct and generally non-negotiable. The bottom line is the trusted guide to the salted board members, squint-eyed bankers and impartial accountants. Basically, this is an effective and debilitating fear tactic to induce an entire sales profession into believing their worth is valued by the day or week of incoming orders. This parental pontification usually comes from a collection of faceless power tools who couldn't sell Tim Hortons coffee to caffeine-thirsty Canadians in Toronto.

The allocation of budgets to sales representatives isn't equitable. Several factors impact a sales rep's potential success. Is their client list vibrant and active, or stagnant and inactive? Does the list predominately feature clients with seasonal or minimal activity? Are the sales hampered by product issues that include inefficiencies or new competitors with striking offers? Additionally, is the manager more focused on socializing with peers rather than actively pursuing practical solutions? Does the manager favor one or two of the other reps, thereby supporting them more?

These factors and many others influence a sales rep's success and can discourage the team's ability to play a fair or mentally healthy game. Several times I've witnessed a general bias that led to unfair removal of active clients from one rep to reward another who had found an easy way to get into the pocket of a senior director. There was surely enough salacious delight in this assignment's distribution to share a knowing smile.

This compromising bias has no place in a professional environment, as it will impact the remuneration, up or down, in any position and on both sides. In effect, budgets can be skewed and unscientific in how they are prescribed. To reward sales reps based on personal preferences or shadowy favors, rather than merit, is a power performance from an unstable manager. This is just one of the complex dynamics that underscores a sales rep's life. The day can start with a tedious, monochromatic staff meeting of no value, a deck of generic lengthy and unintelligible proposals to review or insipid personal distractions from those that have very little to do except intrude on others with their holiday plans or baby stories.

Sales reps face fears each day: The fear of rejection. The fear of loss of income. The fear of their own limitations. The fear of the one co-worker you hate in the office one day becoming your boss.

I believe the biggest fear is irrelevance.

In many ways this is like "imposter syndrome", a root cause that could be related to culture and enhanced by an unsteady job environment. The best way to manage this fear is your willingness to ignore it, by rearranging your ideas of perfection and your focus on negative feelings, and seeing them clearly as irrational. This should minimize the disturbance. Okay, what does that mean? It means to construct a realistic and stable narrative with your business habits. One thing you can do to overcome this debilitating fear is develop a business plan. A business plan that is personal—your map to success. The business plan could entail budgetary goals, client planning for the year and by quarter. This is your plan, not the company's or management. Essentially, you are building a positive sense of purpose. Review it with your manager to provide sustenance to your work. It is an application to move fear and your business outside of emotions and negative thoughts about your worth. It's taking control of your life and expectations, accepting the good and bad equally.

Fear is the child inside, imaginary, destructive and mostly self-manufactured. A lot of what we think and worry about almost never occurs. If we apply the rigors and discipline of excellence in our daily work, we have a chance to succeed on our own terms.

We need to accept failure and see it as the teacher that we learn from the most, even if we loathe him! To get ahead we are taught to conform as we grow into adulthood. We chronicle our experiences with the shaky penmanship of doctrines and issued platitudes, and we compile a collection of events in our lives and friendships amid the droplets of sweat and self-awareness. It is your ego and your frailty fighting each other for first place position. Overcoming fear and building courage is a learned behavior. It is saying "no" instead of "yes" when the fear of rejection overwhelms you, or the fear of not being liked defines you. It's at that moment you become the master of your future, when you allow yourself to choose and not to believe you are chosen.

Be careful of excuses that will hinder your performance by justifying inability or failure. Excuses will block your energy and the courage to face fears. Manufacturing alibis or plotting to shoot your co-worker does not confront fear. Many sales executives fall into the trap of simple-minded thinking by deceiving others and themselves. Unfortunately, survival overshadows competence. There are managers and sales executives whose mindset lies dormant, still in the paleontological period, and having cleverly found usefulness as spies for distrustful directors. These *enfant terrible* slouches occupy valuable space, becoming subjects of office gossip. If

143

you are in sales, you cannot afford to spend your time with gossip groupies who do nothing for your income. Allocating most of your time to clients and prospecting new clients is the best path to a successful career. If you follow this principle, fear will no longer be your survival response.

Harry was someone I once knew in Sydney, a disenchanted sales executive who always saw things negatively. He was the office spy and thrived on office hearsay, whether true or manufactured. This "I-must-find-dirt" malcontent survived because he was anointed as a spy by upper management; they had very little use for him otherwise. Whether what he reported was true or not, didn't matter to him. He developed many conspiratorial office relationships, manifested in scope and science fiction. He built a false personal "brand" as a research expert, which allowed him access to others who felt they needed his expertise. His unlikeable nature and influence grew in proportion to the need for office gossip by his manager. These opportunists often lack skill or merit. It gave him some command and an uneasy sway in the office. It eventually faded when management changed, and his links were forced out.

These dysfunctional individuals do exist in all places – they mate to produce children who later become either politicians, bloggers, or insurance underwriters. (Okay, I'm just imagining that.) We've all worked with someone who trespasses and organizes dissatisfaction, only to hide their business impotence. The "grinning monkeys" are everywhere; they work solely for the reward and a lowly recognition. There is neither ability nor excellence in their work and they thrive on revenge. Like a bloodhound's nose roaming in dirt, piss, and vague directions, they snuffle. They are easily spotted by being overly curious about your business and your time. The best approach is to maintain a friendly demeanor while keeping your distance and safeguarding your time with work habits that produce results.

CHAPTER 22

Your clients should be contagious.

People find safety in distance. The only commitment required is turning on the TV and sharing the couch. Similarly, when you arrive at the office, your biggest commitment is powering up the computer, sipping on a latte and sharing your weekend with co-workers.

In today's business of sales, you still need to go outside to produce business. The modern tools we have access to are invaluable and should be operational for their purpose. Even now with all these tools we have, nothing excites interest as much as a face-to-face meeting. It is repeatedly the backbone of all our relationships. Having minimal contact will make you unrecognizable and shapeless, becoming a brief encounter in a mere moment. This means, your time with a client is proportionate to the business you construct and invest in. In media sales, if you dedicate 90 percent of your work life to a media agency and only 10 percent to their client, this is an unsound business practice. Over-relying on an agency will diminish your autonomy and then you become vulnerable if your "friend" leaves the agency; it will take time to make a new friend. Strong client relationships have always been synonymous with long-term success. If you refuse to build client relationships, it's like walking with one leg instead of two; you need the two, agency and client. Relationships with the agency are important and should not be underestimated.

Another reason you should know the client personally and nurture your face-to-face meetings is that these meetings can expose you to new opportunities that only direct-client engagement can offer. If you are working in a media group that is not the top dog in ratings and perception, then it will negatively affect your financial stability. When I was in sales, I was always client focused. I made it a mission to build strong client relationships. I recall when I was at a business function in Melbourne, where a major international retailer was unveiling their product line and marketing plans for the year to all media companies in Australia. I had developed a professional relationship with the national marketing director of this company. At that time, I was selling, promoting and building a startup media network. We were not exactly top of mind with clients or agencies as we were new to the country. My relationship with this client was one of mutual respect.

After three or four visits with him and his team, they decided to try my new product. Their current agency just went along with it; we were too small to be a threat or even noticeable. If it weren't for the encouragement of the client, they would not have considered us. The major media companies in Australia were in attendance at this function in Melbourne, which took place in the lobby of the opulent Regent Theatre. This retailer carried considerable weight in the industry, in size and reputation, and was in the top 10 of media advertising spenders in Australia. I managed to grab a few minutes of his time before the event began. We had a brief conversation about business, though it was nothing of profound substance. As the lobby cleared, attendees from the media industry found their seats. The first part of the presentation involved introductions and colorful images on a big screen. Finally, the gentleman I had spoken with in the lobby appeared onstage. Minutes into his speech, he mentioned my name and company, speaking of our conversation to the audience as if we were good friends. I was stunned to hear my name echo throughout the theatre, not expecting this—it was surreal. During intermission, a person from one of the major TV networks seemed impressed enough to jokingly ask how much I paid for the mention. In a more serious (no, really) tone, he wanted to know how I knew him.

I knew him, and he knew me, because I made it my mission to meet with clients, shaking hands with those who invest in me. This person from the TV network, who always managed to secure a sizeable portion of the TV ad revenue, had never met this client. His company worked exclusively through their agency. Later, getting into my car, I wondered how much money he let slip through his fingers by maintaining distance while collaborating with his agency.

Keeping distance from the client is never an ideal way to develop a meaningful business relationship, except if your interest is with the local barista at the café down the street. When you rely on others to control your interactions and the convulsive use of objects such as advertising agencies, tedious emails, online social media and inopportune global viruses, all this chaos overwhelmingly influences or disrupts your personal autonomy and communication. You become a bystander to practical rapport, thereby shrinking your business success and limiting your personal connections.

The distance that I'm talking about is in the form of expensive software to keep the sales rep in the office, and too many meetings, which – again – keep the sales reps in the office. It is ass-backwards to place all your livelihood bets on a donkey in the Kentucky Derby or Melbourne Cup. Such passive activities will surely fail. With people, we can never see every facet of an individual. In the same way, looking only at the "front" of a business, our hopes and promises with those few we solicit or befriend, will remain flat. Any offer you put on the table is as one dimensional as that tablet you carry from the cafes to your bed.

Any employer who has accepted the new business paradigm—whether out of reluctance or enthusiasm—by straying from established operational standards is prioritizing fleeting trends over essential productivity. This shift often results in a workforce that is only partially engaged. The phenomenon echoes the leisure suit fad of the 1970s, which was worn both at the office and casual gatherings, reflecting a split in its intended purpose.

This duality creates a tension between respect and functionality. It manifests in various ways, such as the management of client relationships by external agents. These outside forces dictate your team's activities, even influencing basic interactions like a simple greeting. Many managers, intimidated by these agents, surrender control and allow them to dictate team behavior and access to clients. This is a troubling compromise that undermines both respect and efficacy in the workplace.

The evolving business landscape these days restricts direct-client meetings, reshaping how client interactions are managed and controlled. Agencies, rather than clients, may be assigned to sales representatives, leading to indirect relationships with those who control the budget. This shift blurs the focus, as businesses cultivate familiarity with an intermediary agent rather than the decision-maker. As a result, products are often adapted and shaped to the preferences of these agencies, which may have broader market dealings. I have seen this happen, where the product is an ideal match, but the trading dynamics become as complex as "extraterrestrial" bargaining. Products are tailored and dressed to suit the needs and desires of intermediary agencies, rather than always aligning with direct needs. A creative idea can supplant a media platform in pushing a vain program to win an industry award. There is the fear of losing business by not conforming to the marketplace; it is deeply ingrained in the entire business of solicitation. Media groups are losing money because they have not relied on their real power – a large audience – or leveraged enough strength. They are the teenager without the keys, failing to unlock a high-performance car. It is not a new, upgraded "millennial" way of doing business. It is simply one decisive step away from doing best sales practices. We clock our steps on smart watches to ensure a good cardio workout. We should clock our outdoor meetings to calculate and gauge a healthy business mindfulness (and a good cardio workout).

You may see a fitness deficit or opportunity in your business that you overlooked. Great sales reps keep to a daily "fitness" routine pertaining to their business; one that is unequalled and extraordinary with genuine client engagement.

By keeping busy for the sake of being busy, with nonessentials that steal your time, such as computer stalking or nosying up clients on social media, you exhaust both your time and your day. All of this to achieve the aim of trying to look busy and capable. The 5 p.m. beers cannot come soon enough. Hey, no client appointments, but boy, did I have a busy day. My fingers ache from pounding the keys instead of the streets, and so does my head with worry—and, naturally, no client responses! I love sales!

So, as a boss, or an employee, how do you combat the *provocateur* time waster, referred to as email, or the snoop in the office? The battle is hugely both internal and external. Clearly though, the blame is on you, if you allow your work time to be interrupted by others. The best way to begin your day is by shutting down the time wasters. To ready yourself with corrective and positive activity, and that includes prospecting for new business. If you are not that elite sales rep with a big bank account and big clients, your days are being compromised or swallowed up by dreaming and praying. That is the time when you need to evaluate whether sales is the profession for you. If you are one of those people who constantly need to convince everyone of everything, no matter how trite, then great, stay in the game. If you prefer to read an enjoyable book alone or watch a documentary about the speed of multi-legged insects, bypassing a dinner party, then a career change should be considered. Sales is high energy, with high expectations and highly interpersonal activity. Spending your time in the office in front of a computer is not selling. Some might consider it planning or building a case for your product, but it is not selling. In my experience the most competent and successful sales representatives are those that excel in client networking. Their entertainment expenses typically rank among the highest. The differentiator between low-performing and high-performing reps often lies within their expense reports—these reports serve as a crystal ball, telling numerous stories. The key factor that determines success is the extent of client contact. There is no magical sorcery in the art of selling—only common sense and a genuine desire to engage.

You won't find it in your manager's office or a scripted phone introduction. This arbitration of client distance is begrudgingly accepted by management when the agency determines how many reps are allowed to enter their kingdom. The fear of losing access to the agency is real and problematic but not realistic. Leave the more enlightened work of meeting clients with a steady hand – one that may be slapped by an agent – to the ambitious, inventive and energetic. There is too much at stake to expose your time and business to the silliness of imaginary outcomes. If you look up, you'll see the sky has no boundaries or sick weary eyes; there are just open possibilities.

I was tasked by the CEO of a company with the building of a fresh team of sales representatives I called "Hunters". Their sole role was to bring in new business—not a job for the faint-hearted. They had the toughest role in the company. Although we were a separate sales division, we were a part of the overall sales effort. Over time the managers on the other side developed a strange fixation on my team. Their mere presence and fruitful activity seemed to irritate them. A previous team, similar to the Hunters, had eventually disbanded. The simplistic reasoning was that all sales representatives should fall under the control of one person, specifically the national sales director. This was typical of a power grab and short-sighted thinking. The Hunters were creative, mostly working outside the office to meet with prospective clients, and they were also brave and independently minded. Unfortunately, but not surprisingly, a few top-level managers and directors lost their purpose and focused on the chaos they created for personal gain, not the company's. They failed to see the bottom line by focusing on crude politics. There may be opposition by outside and inside forces that will discourage you, but you must find a way to make your business whole and distinguishable from the pack who are devoted to a prayer book, not a powerful force.

According to B.F. Skinner, a well-known behavioral psychologist, our behavior is shaped by positive and negative reinforcement. The increased probability that encouragement through repetitive action will create a consequence of fearlessness and success. With negative reinforcement we increase the probability of failure or mediocrity. This shaping begins during childhood and continues through our growing years at home, school and work. I have trained talented sales reps who lacked confidence and moved from job to job, mainly because of a dysfunctional work environment where the predictability of "doormat management's" vulnerability to outside influence, and the characterizations of threats and weak thinking, impacted on their business. This cultural sales facility has become inflexible as the sales organization is increasingly trained to trust the persuasive enforcer, whoever that may be, that only serves to banish you and your product to oblivion. The drive to push forward may undermine both the bottom line and the team's morale, creating a business environment where independent thinking and action are discouraged. This type of dangerous and managerial mangling kills the very soul of performance. It encourages unethical behavior by fostering "hide-and-seek" personality traits and work avoidance. In addition, you will find desk-chained sales reps creating elaborately plausible excuses, which carry them to the end of each day. The excuse is like an unplanned heart attack while running on a treadmill. As you wait for the ambulance to arrive, your co-workers, knowing it will come, will wait for word of your demise. The message is: don't become an addict of failure by sustaining fraudulent business activities of your "self". There is nothing illegal about hiding the very definition of an unremarkable career. There is nothing to be gained either. Make it your mission to meet and build relationships with clients. It will provide you with extraordinary confidence and power in the ability to control your business and income. The alternative is to let some kid at an agency tell you who you can and cannot see. You must demand more of yourself to operate in today's skittish business environment. The *status quo* is not your friend if you must continually fight the fatigue of capturing a sale, or anything that resembles a sale. The voice of the individual is powerful, and you should ensure your voice is heard when you sense you are being crushed by commerce without a brain.

CHAPTER 23

Presentations and proposals advice.

Smug married couples who have everything in life share a common thread among social researchers. They are the truth sayers, telling all what we should want. What we should purchase. When to have kids. How to raise kids, and who we should marry. They look at our lives through the lens of a black and white kaleidoscope projecting polarization and splitting images without color or nuance. When they speak, it's like a sermon, enlisting help from traditional values and the latest science babble. It is incomprehensible; a televangelist speaking in tongues would be considered more coherent.

People and programs design a composite of a typical person in a Barbie-Land-type world. The truth is there is no reality as a typical client or person in these come-as-you-are days. The human mind is emotional, negative and irrational, as well as positive, intellectual and curious. That means hashtag everything: #sales plans, #computer generated data,

#colorful advertising proposals, #emails, #following influencers, #CRM software, #crystal ball, #happy Microsoft, #happy Bill Gates, #research.

Demographics are neatly packaged to explain our motivation, structure and the habits of humankind; media organisations eat this stuff up like vegans chomping on smashed avocado on toast.

I'm going to add more about the usefulness of client relationships. The most valuable currency in sales is client relationships. Instead, we allow a faceless computer clairvoyant ruin the potential of a frank and open possibility. The most meaningful conversation between the sales representative and the client should not be a maneuver of simulated technology with childlike graphs and numbers. As a tool it has its function, and it can show a sliver of sophistication at the hands of an eager sales rep, perfecting the font and images. The analogy I use is—*The carpenter is not the hammer.* The advisor is not the cloud-based presentation. What is the best presentation tool? *You.* If the sales culture in your company is primarily weighted upon, and dependent on, administrative technology, then your business is a well-dressed vagrant roaming from boring slide to painfully boring slide, begging for spare change.

Clients will not necessarily need to know how clever your design and graphic skills are when watching an *ADHD Venn*. I believe the client would rather hear more about themselves, their business and how you can achieve their objectives. That means let them talk endlessly about themselves. Even by allowing them to brag about their Land Rover. All you must do is convince them that your company is the right fit and if it is, it's the beginning of a worthwhile business introduction that could lead to a solid and resourceful long-term relationship. Leave the formulated sugar and suppress the cartoon characters for the kid's cereal boxes. A real adult solution outflanks any digitized analytic component even if it is complete with humorus memes, and juvenile streaming animation. They never connect with any real meaning, except that it is fun to look at it. It's a specialty in corporate suicide to awaken to mediocrity and nursery rhymes.

We copy other people's ideas! An original concept is only embraced when somebody else does it first, and then others claim it as their own. We all know original ideas are formidable and difficult to comprehend in our super-charged world. Copying is expediency. Copying is familiar. Copying is comfortable for lazy minds. Many proposals I have dissected for media sales reps are depressingly generic, overly price emphasized and a repeat of the company's attributes, *ad nauseam*. It is media-centric, not client-centric. It's basically how to impress ourselves. It's an inward-mirrored ego, not an outward engagement. What we should aim for is a wide-open path, working alongside the client or agency to build a deck together in a vigorous and productive cooperative collaboration. Nothing bulky or time consuming for both. Any person of influence has deadlines and a busy schedule to oversee. Begin by drafting a relevant and desired buyer/seller alignment outline of where you want to go. This will enable you to have a greater success hit rate, by defining the reality of their needs to the final execution, bringing clarity and purpose.

Delivering a solution that goes beyond mere aesthetics and superficial cost analysis is essential to making your mark meaningful. Approach every proposal with tangible, actionable results that set you apart from competition. Something that is specific, leveraging creativity to make it stand out in the crowded media space. Spend time to think on how you can move the needle closer to "yes" with the synergy of mirroring the value proposition closer towards a client's point of view. Throw everything of value – and only value – on the table and then get tactical. The courage to talk to clients in real life, not real time, without gimmicks or synthetic sourcing, will go a long way towards building your credibility and your company's higher standard of communication. You want to sit at the table, not serve it.

It is time to replace your crystal balls with bison balls. I'll say it a thousand times—*nothing* replaces or beats connecting with a client on a human face-to-face level. It may sound unconventional in the current world of Zoom meetings, but head-to-head technology is not a viable contender or an alternative. In my experience (and my experience is global) the human connection is more productive, more creative and more spontaneous with solutions than all the quirkily-named social networks combined. When you finally get that meeting, and you are sitting happily and politely in front of a client, why take out a nondescript computer to present your product thereby losing the powerful testimony of what you're selling? You are both looking at the screen and missing important body language cues and non-verbal facial expressions. It's a form of not really paying attention in the presence of the client. You may have been taught and conditioned to be a Steve Jobs or any big-name speaker you follow, larger than life on a big commanding screen. You may dress up in super cool black and wear clean white sneakers. But we are all mere mortals – we fidget in our chair, sliding our fingers around a thin sheet of glass, having foreplay with the screen. The client's movements and yours are jerky and shifting behind us in front of a fake backdrop, exposing our desire to be lounging on a sandy tropical beach. Or the top of a forehead is all that's seen because of a misplaced camera. This is monotonous stage setting which interrupts the flow of conversation. It is not selling or engagement. We hang up, and the client is onto another forgettable Zoom meeting.

Another losing format we cling to are 2D-shaped gimmicks or thought bubbles in proposals covered in thick large font that you would normally find in the colourful table mats placed on tables at low-brow restaurants. It is paramount that the focus remains on you – not on a photo of you or a bunch of words poorly fit on a screen with a thin, metallic-sounding speaker. Engagement is a sharp tool, and if you are who you really think you are as a sales scholar, you'll cultivate that skill and become a virtuoso in the finest sales techniques.

If you are like many others you'll go along with every ill-suited idea, then submit a generic proposal to a client. And one day you'll wake up and learn that your proposal is more bin-worthy than recycled cans and bottles.

* If the client doesn't know who you are, it is
likely that it will go in the bin.

* If your proposal doesn't offer a solution or match their criteria, it is likely it will go in the bin.

* If your proposal lacks credibility, it will likely go in the bin.

* If your proposal doesn't provide real value, it is likely it will go in the bin.

* If your proposal is emailed to a client or agency who doesn't know you, it is likely it will go in the bin

* If your proposal is...... {now think of other ways} ... it is likely to go in the bin.

Consider, if you please, these steps to build a strong bin-less proposal.

1. Do your research first. (I know I have made fun of research, but it works where it's needed). To provide value, your proposal must make retail sense. It must address the client's needs, current objectives and concerns with a strong value proposition.

2. Your proposal should open with a summary of the contents inside, which will create a familiar read from the beginning. This is not a summary of the proposal. It's a summary of reasons why the client should buy your product. It should be written to get the tone of the proposal right. To feign off any selling anxiety that the client may internalize. If they know up front what is being presented, they can relax and the communication and offering will flow much easier.

3. Tell them why the client will be interested in your product.

4. Create a mental picture first of how the client will benefit and how it fits and visualize the interaction.

5. It should include a call to action and a time frame, and if a transaction is included, it should have a due date to by which to receive a decision.

6. When it's completed, role-play the presentation with a colleague, or a friend. It will strengthen your voice. Or do a table-read to hear how it flows.

It is not an information pack, containing details of your product, but a financial investment recommendation, lightly covering how your product's attributes align with the prospect's goals. All your proposals should be client focused while also focusing on value. Show evidence that you are providing solutions to their objectives and stay away from repeating media talk that is condescending. The closing should have happened earlier, in previous meetings. The proposal is the culmination of the total selling activity, and the proposal is the final sign off for both parties. Therefore, it must be crafted with the right number of specifics and positive talking points. As a final check, before you submit your proposal/deck, or whatever you want to call it, remove all irrelevant elements and redundant graphics. Keep it tight and easy to understand. The presentation isn't going to sell it, you already have. Practice speaking and answering objections in a calm manner that elicits trust and confidence. Keep in mind, no one likes to spend money. If someone is asked to spend money no matter how small the fraction, the objections will stack up in succession. On the other hand, does anyone object to free bonuses or a free meal? Do not show weakness by offering concessions or a reduction of price if you sense pullback. Stay in control. Immerse yourself in the deal by remaining committed to your offer. Place more trust in yourself and your product before you go down the "commodity road" of hard bargaining. Ultimately, it's your authentic presence that will answer the clients' objectives and influence an affirmative outcome.

CHAPTER 24

Selling is as cool as jazz.

Selling can be cool.

Place the brass horn to your mouth and start blowing with a new vocabulary and expression like John Coltrane when he manipulated and transformed his music into a spiritual delivery from way above and inside.

Sales is jazz, and beautifully discordant, while mostly improvisational. Sales is not strumming a perfectly tuned guitar, sitting and grinning on a rustic porch playing harmony chords. The notes of sales flow freely in their unpredictability and deviations, creating a unique pitch.

In the constantly evolving sales world, there are varying degrees of perceptions and permutations. A one-act, regimented and always-the-same sales delivery is limited and dated. With clients there are many different personality types, each erratic, some presuming and all mostly robust and accountable. This is one important reason why you must know the "notes" and be able to demonstrate a performance delivery to fit the occasion. The act of presentation is another sales instrument that requires practice and improvisation, like playing the saxophone. It will enable you to allow creativity and curiosity to flourish, and thus free you to unlearn the tired routine habits that inescapably hold you back. You will crave the human interaction and enjoy the reciprocation. You'll want more.

Charismatic, award-winning actors rehearse assiduously and study meticulously for weeks each time they grace a live audience on stage. The intensity, focus and passion for their highly competitive craft is obvious, and the result when practiced with care is inspirational. The ability to accept direction, rehearse a script and be aware of the importance of movement and speech is paramount in good acting. It is the cousin to sales in all forms of presentations. It runs parallel to the demands of your competence and communication skills. At every new business meeting, the sales executive is on stage. The motto then is "be prepared or be accidental".

There are professions where accountability is the standard practice by law and vigilantly regulated – doctors, dentists and lawyers. Each of these highly- regarded professions require a license update every 1-3 years to be bona fide. Any profession that is recognised by a governing body for a working license that can be quickly revoked or suspended will grasp the seriousness and necessity of skill upgrades, scrupulous behavior, and professional development. Especially when health, liberty and finances are a factor. In the competitive world of sales, people embark on markedly different paths—some opting for professionalism and integrity, while others traverse an opportunistic road with shallow promises. Intriguingly, the latter often thrives, favored in environments where managers prioritize the illusion of confidence over genuine competence. The sales landscape lacks a stringent regulatory authority to revoke industry licenses, account portfolios or extravagant expense privileges. Instead, the sole arbiter of this is the sales manager whose gaze is always fixed on the bottom line. In such an ecosystem, ethics and truthfulness become fluid concepts, swayed by subjective judgements rather than objective standards. Managers are aligned with results over accountability and ethics. If our profession is not regulated and the industry goes along with the expected twist or exaggeration of promises, it reflects the complexities and general acceptance of a profession that is inadequately trained. I'm not saying that charisma universally overshadows ability, but there are a lot of polished, toothy sales reps who have no other experience except the monkey's grin.

Let me go back to role-play and something else called curiosity. It is at its core a practical "learning tree" that allows us a continual evaluation of our knowledge and skills, strengthening our verbal skills to wrestle with tough questions from inflexible merchants and their savvy agents. When skills are planted in the past – for the past, and not for the future – you will never adapt to change from random and changeable events, or unexpected client displacement or shrinkage. Business is all about expansion. When you stop learning or evaluating your skills and growth, it will kill the very soul of performance. You may find you're chained to your desk and email, secured and insecure, completely relying on two or three big-spending clients. To understand where you are going, you'll need plenty of curiosity to get you there. The conversation in your mind should fascinate and free you to unlearn the tired, routine habits that inescapably hold you back. In time you will desire human interaction outside the comfort of your home office.

Curiosity is indispensable in the business of sales, as in the business of life. You begin and emerge by asking questions and then by asking more questions. Take plenty of notes at meetings, whether it is face to face or virtual. These notes will later provide necessary clues when triggering your memory. It also shows the client you are interested and engaged with them as people. How do children grow and develop? Aside from a healthy and loving family life, a balanced diet and clean environment, curiosity is also an important element. Losing the wonder of curiosity marks the beginning of a regression from expression and interest. This ultimately makes you old and ossified. The outcome – or the bottom line – becomes your cynical partner, and in that waltz the music fades, leaving you a solitary figure trapped in the past under a dull, lonesome light. Though poetic, it rings true. Curiosity elevates client relationships to a deeper level of understanding, growth and reflection. It fuels your learning, adding an excitement and passion to negotiations. Your questions will carry greater weight, authority and thoughtfulness.

Communicating within the client's language sphere will unlock new opportunities, leading to the discovery of a new language—the language of genuine collaboration. The path to connectedness with your client will feel natural, facilitating problem-solving without distrust or defense. It also aligns the client closer to you and your product. You become more relatable, and your product offering more appealing.

In Chicago I had a lunch meeting with five sales reps and their manager. The sales representative at the lunch had a problem that she needed to work out, and she wanted to discuss it with the group. She disclosed that she couldn't

170

understand why the agency of this particular client was only interested in internet advertising, as opposed to traditional radio advertising. She continued by saying "the agency doesn't like the radio format, even though we know this agency uses radio for other clients". When I asked her why, she responded by repeating "the client doesn't like radio". I thought this may have accompanied the reason why the agency did not favor radio in this case. I asked her why the client was against radio advertising? She commented by saying "radio advertising was too expensive". I continued to ask her why. She said, "they would rather place their ads alongside specific programs". When I again asked why, she said, "they like reaching a smaller, but well-targeted audience". Another why from me. She paused and didn't respond this time. I watched how her brain was searching for an answer. The manager at that point chuckled, staring at me like he grasped where I was going with my excessive probing. The manager realized I was persistently questioning her with "whys" to assess her understanding of both the agency and client decision-making processes. In other words, had she asked enough questions. Was she capable of huddling with them to build a strong case for radio?

The buyer's decision process is complicated and not what we instantly perceive. Asking "why" repeatedly can lead down the road to discovery. Finding the real reasons, in this case asking why they are an advocate for a particular media platform, is a conversation builder. After my little exercise, she realized her questioning was incomplete. By accepting their bias with very little query, she found that it ultimately led the "art of persuasion" to a dead end. How do you push back an argument convincingly if you ask single-answer questions that go nowhere?

Receiving unexpected meeting invitations that make you feel honored and fortunate will lead to the domestication of being overly grateful and overly accommodating. This vain gratitude will ensure you will not ask too many questions; you will sit straight and be polite and ineffective—because you want to be liked. You want any seat that is given to you at the table. Your kindness is like sweet butter corn at a farmer's market. A happy, edible vegetable that everyone will enjoy. Asking relevant questions (contrary to what some reps may believe) is not combative, unless you execute your delivery as an investigation, like a pompous prosecutor. It should open the mindscape of the clients' thoughts and direction. The question becomes how your offering could help achieve goals by engaging in value, not price. It will reveal what the missing links are to further the clients' interest. In so many cases it's a battle of perception and costs. Similar to a long-standing religious tradition that's hard to let go, the perception of your product resembles a revered religious artifact. This leads to obscured opinions and hinders rational discussion.

The buyer may believe they know your product like they know God. By pushing hard against the immovable, you will find there are other barriers, big and small, that need to be cleared first. An upgrade of information with support from your company may be just the communication tool that delivers real interest and a "come to Jesus" moment. Follow the lead of children. Asking questions helps the child with validation and confirmation. It's a big play for interaction and understanding. Adults stop asking questions when they become apathetic, overconfident or just adults.

As a wise person – some say Einstein - once wrote, "The definition of insanity is doing the same thing over and over again and expecting a different result"

There are plenty of insane companies.

The only way to get out of that repetitive hole is to ask "why" exhaustively. Take off the mask of expert and learn something new about yourself, about your product and about the client's business. You can only accomplish a fresh way of thinking by asking questions that will get you closer to the client's objectives.

I've been in countless meetings where the sales representative would brag – I mean *talk* – about their product endlessly without coming up for air, wasting a perfect opportunity to learn something new. It's like trying to make out in the back seat of a diesel 4x4, while driving over ridges and rocks at top speed.

Beware of the know-it-all in yourself and your hard rock ideology. Ask "why".

CHAPTER 25

Semiotics and communication.

We live in a culture of disposability, from relationships to training tools, to pop business concepts and many other things beyond our wildest imagination. That is, until we become brave enough to communicate from the inside first, if that is even possible when surrounded by the noise of our desires. The first place we go to get inside ourselves is meditation.

The popularity and activity of modern meditation is conflicted. The inner self is pieced together to fit loosely like a warm blanket, providing a resting place. This temporarily replaces the external world of commitment by shortcutting the ancient and serious introspection, requiring devotion and uncovering nothingness in achieving inner peace. It takes a pledge of lifelong hard work and sacrifice. Unlike the modern enthusiast sitting cross-legged in a sunny park or a dimly lit room, this quiet state of vain and unremarkable inner focus aims to impress, digest and regress, like others seeking spiritual status. Advertisers and marketers follow these would-be-pilgrims, selling lines of loose-fitting, meditation clothing, singing bowls and cruelty-free fragrances that provide an air of superiority. These "guru gadgets" purchased by modern-day spiritual seekers, are meant to help answer life's big questions and provide self-identity amidst their busy careers and busy social schedules. It is not unlike the angry cyclist, dressed like a professional racer, shouting self-righteous invectives at SUVs carrying tired travellers. What exactly are they communicating?

The tendency to adopt surface-level solutions and appearances over genuine internal understanding and introspection, contrasts sharply with the consumer-driven popular mindset surrounding modern day practices. In the context of selling, the sales rep often falls into the trap of quick-fix solutions, focusing only on the external trappings or gimmicks that promise instant results. Instead, they need to be encouraged to understand their clients by reflecting empathy, commitment and genuineness rather than a surface-level charm.

Our society is a sweeping montage of outlaw men and women, trapped in the invention of used ideas, transparent by a narcissistic outgrowth of stunted information. There are professionals who show the world via their podcasts how knowledgeable and interesting they are. They globe-trot social media with excitable eyes, insidious words and finger pointing, while their connections and growing subscriber list validate the wasteland we currently live in.

We consume our lives with pretend communication, partly from a psychedelic hangover carried over from the alphabet generations to the complaining, geriatric baby boomers. We're using our brain and hurriedness to find temporary solutions. We seek support from celebrated podcast personalities and counterfeit TV nerds. It's all there for us to digest like a drippy, over-priced Big Mac in our wanting hands. We ask friends and business associates to cut and paste ideas and thought bubbles to distribute as proof of performance. We dance online with our unusual human pets. We perpetuate trending culture fads with rehash-ties to our baby-self or selfies. It's exhausting how much attention we crave. There must be so much more than the electricity connecting of our hungry lust to the poster friends and job networking we turn on every day.

Communication is actively listening, observing closely and not necessarily doing; it is also creating an image that others will like or share for an instant grab. It's about being genuine with yourself and with others. The internet is the open-range zoo with gorillas chasing butterflies for sport and pleasure. We are much bigger than the headlines that destroy empathy and thinking, or our strange pursuit of nothing that can be touched or felt. Every day we watch and listen, reading the news for enlightenment and truth, and seeking out leaders of genuine character. Every day we are disappointed. Every day we look for answers from our friends and co-workers while they're trying to clean up their own shit. We begin to think this is reality and a composite image of what our life looks like. Mostly, we are driven by what we believe people want or expect from us, whether it's in the execution of work, or simply in the outward way we dress. Men and women with nose rings and colorful tattoos, like an action comic book, are so incredibly conservative, communicating the need to be accepted. To belong somewhere in the middle of a search for something. Followers aren't leaders. Leaders aren't followers. As the prolific singer/songwriter Richard Thompson astutely pointed out "She's got everything a girl might need, she's a tribal animal, yes indeed. But she hasn't got a bone through her nose". Or perhaps she does.

It takes courage to communicate your true language, to change and to act with conviction against a norm that may not work for you. Or you can continue muddling along in a softly lit room, slightly pornographic, full of desires and incompleteness, hoping to attract other incomplete, vulnerable persons to stroke.

We have the power and ability to communicate. Have you noticed how that happens innately when you listen to the music you love? It touches you deeply and you never question how or why, you just sing along. It is ebullient, the timeless language of sound and soul. At times it is quiet, or explosively loud. It's a freer, honest form of expression. It is also intimate. It's one of the few intimate forms of communication that you can share with the public without being judged with disapproval or thrown in jail. Again, communication thrives more on the spontaneous and genuine exchange of ideas than on a pseudo-intellectual platform that simulates predatory headlines. The act of engaging in futile arguments on social media reflects this issue. I'm not leveling criticism specifically at social media, yet it seems to have replaced honest communication, becoming the progenitor of incomplete exchanges. Unfortunately, it is where many people source their information today. It appeals to the lazy and crude, stifling thinking and individualistic ideas. It resembles a gunslinger without bullets or purpose, while making IT nerds and business leaders wealthy. It distorts genuine opinions. Does it even matter that your essential knowledge consists of unremarkable stories, echoing in line with those barking similar beliefs of custom-made vanity. Or that it's probably not true or substantial, even when your friends or neighbors agree. It's the babble of the masses and the disease of incompleteness that overwhelm and shorten thought. Our deceit is that we genuinely believe we fully communicate inside a screen, laptops and research. It is common that we've accepted this unquestioned delivery method of communication, which has now become the foundation of our humanness and the decisions that are the core of our beliefs. It supports our secular lives, our increasing biases and dressed-up falseness at a costume party. In life, as in sales, we must learn courage. The courage to be who we really are. To say what we know and what we mean. To be decisive and not be thinly influenced by a chorus of lost voices who will only wish you to conform to what they expect.

In Tokyo, I worked closely with an astute businessman, who was our national sales manager in Japan. We reviewed operating procedures and how best to marry the unique culture of his world with the western drive of our company's expectations. Our conversation was positive and meaningful until I asked him to start "thinking" about his business moving forward and where he thinks it could go. I emphasized the word 'think'. He looked at me with a concerned expression and said "Bill, in Japan we aren't taught to think —we are taught to do".

Those words remained with me throughout my sales training career. How the cultural contrast in "thinking" is perceived. That in Japan, for example, people are taught more to act than to think independently. Thinking was something I assumed everyone naturally did all the time as an automatic, universal process, varying with how deep or shallow the skill. A word like "think" to me is like a familiar bird on your lawn. You have seen it many times and you know what animal it is, but you may not know its species or understand where it came from or where it's going. It's a word that encompasses many meanings, from the cerebral that is obvious to the emotional that is more complex.

The multifaceted and deep nature of thinking is, just like the bird, its true nature and is more profound and complex than it appears. I offer this insight based on what I've witnessed with sales reps parroting the mannerisms of others to advance their careers.

The businessman from Tokyo took it differently, as I asked him to recreate his universe. My initial reaction was, "Okay, so here's what I want you to do". Problem solved! It wasn't that easy.

In the West, the emphasis has been central, with a strong cultural focus on independent thought and inner strength. This contrasts sharply with the Eastern culture, where workers have traditionally been more defined by their loyalty to a team, and their ability to conform to external pressure. The inner strength that I spoke about earlier is a recurring theme throughout my experiences of training people from different cultures on how values must be maintained within their culture, and not an import of my mindset. The importance of genuine understanding is in the value of using different approaches and languages to problem-solve. You'll be far more effective in building a fully whole business, and forming wonderful interpersonal relationships, if you uncover the freer part of yourself that employers or peers can never convert or exploit. Be honest and allow yourself to take more risks. Look at the vastness of your professional life, as opposed to the context of fastening on a one-dimensional description of how things should be done. It's communication on a visceral level that will give you a stronger backbone if you rock down the highway of unexplored terrain, where you are commissioned to break free from a tight mindset of prescribed habits.

CHAPTER 26

A first date or a business lunch?

It takes 'know how' and table etiquette to arrange utensils on a dining table. The knowledge of what is or isn't important and how to order them. The plate, the forks, the spoon and the knives all placed and assembled in the order of use. This would be the case if you're fine dining or enrolled in an etiquette school. In sales everyone is hungry. An unusual amount of time is spent deciding where to eat. Many sales reps who are aiming to impress will choose a fine-dining experience over the cafeteria-style takeout, but once you can identify the difference between ketchup and a Béarnaise sauce, you'll never miss the gulf between a schooner and an aperitif.

There are no obvious lines that invite hospitality and its distinctions to its destination. If you are going to entertain an important client, and make a considerable investment, then make it memorable. Abandon activities that are slight and a waste of everyone's time. Read the player to suit the purpose;

it might be a kingly type who is at home and comfortable in a 5-star hotel environment or a grungy creative who is just skateboarding to the latest edgy taco establishment. Never assume all clients have all the same needs and expectations. There are no consistent rules with clients and how to gastronomically win them over. Some gush over a fine red pinot, while another may be equally excited over a green smoothie with sprinkled nuts and grains.

Some of my most successful deals were struck in modest cafés, with the details sketched on a paper napkin. It's not always necessary to offer grand gestures in every sales action if a strong relationship has already been established. Let's not forget, it is essential for a potential client to feel comfortable with your venue choice. I have seen media planners, rough around the edges, invited to a lunch at exquisite restaurants with highly skilled chefs and dramatic ambiance. They often stare at the menu with uncertainty, like a toddler gazing at a pictureless book. It could leave them overwhelmed and feeling uncomfortably indebted by the royal treatment. For the sales rep who might regularly dine in such luxury, the distinction between everyday eateries and a five-star experience might not be as apparent.

The importance of understanding your client's comfort zone and preferences cannot be overstated. By being attentive to these details, you begin to create an environment where the client feels at ease, which can lead to more productive conversations. The need for thoughtful consideration over habitual *razzle-dazzle* ensures you're aligned with the client's comfort and that you appreciate the perimeters – either wide or narrow – of the client's expectations. This leads to why lunches and entertaining clients are essential and should be an "artery" to the heart of your selling. It's a time without disturbances for you and the client to get to know each other as humans, without the badge of your title or the crude language of business jargon. Avoid bringing your laptop or any proposals that require decisions or overthinking. Remove the tight-fitted, cautious mask, and let your client discover another, hopefully interesting, side of you. You don't need to remind them or hold them hostage to a nagging, long-winded dissertation on how wonderful you and your product are. Instead, try the unique habits of listening and learning. When both parties are engaged and conversation is flowing like fine wine pouring into crystal glasses, you're on your way to establishing a robust relationship. Then you are in the process of effectively building trust and rapport; this applies in both business and personal settings.

On another level, you might face an awkward situation when a business and personal lunch meeting conflate. A very attractive young woman worked for me as a senior sales representative. For a long time, our company had been trying to secure a meeting with a large spending advertiser who was unfamiliar with our product. She came into my office, excited to report the news that she had secured an appointment with this client, and even better, a lunch meeting for their first encounter. We celebrated with high fives, and she gave me an itinerary outlining her presentation. I asked how she managed to arrange the lunch since this client had always been evasive. She felt her persistence had paid off. On the day of the meeting, we reviewed the specifics of her verbal pitch to the client. I felt that this lunch could be the turning point in our relationship with him and our company. I couldn't have asked for a better representative – she was bright, intuitive and persuasive.

After her lunch meeting, she came directly to my office, behaving dreamily but with a wide smile. I assumed it went well. She explained how he liked our product and could find ways to use it, all of which sounded positive—until she mentioned he had paid for the lunch. I looked at her with disappointment. She became confused and asked what was wrong. I said "That wasn't a business meeting; it was a date. By allowing him to pay for lunch, you unknowingly relinquished your power by submitting to vanity. The company provides all sales reps with a generous entertainment allowance to ensure your authority and position are never compromised. You gave your power away because you thought he liked you and you were seduced by that idea. He wasn't interested in what you were selling; he was interested in you".

She was visibly upset with my interpretation of her lunch and repeatedly insisted I was wrong. Allowing the client to pay had shifted the balance of power. To add nuance within the dynamics of the workplace, if this was an established client with an established relationship with the sales rep, who pays for the meal wouldn't have been as critical. She returned to my office a couple of hours later looking listless. She was carrying a printed copy of an email he sent describing their meeting, enthusiastically suggesting that they meet up for another lunch meeting. In his email he expressed no interest in or mention of our company. She finally agreed with me, that she had allowed herself to be misrepresented by what she interpreted as just a sense of connection. In the end, I removed this client from her list by mutual consent. She didn't want to be placed in harm's way or have her professionalism compromised in any way. I knew we wouldn't hear from him again, and that was fine with me. In time, after he left his company, we were able to start fresh and open a dialogue with boundaries, eventually securing their business.

CHAPTER 27

A big chapter... you figure it out.

Conflicts organize our life in business. Without conflict there is no meaningful growth or direction, and your work becomes a roomful of more of the same, resulting in stunted growth. The choices that conflict deliberates are made in many places, including solemn boardrooms and in the busy hallways, bouncing off casual conversations. Decisions are made with intense scrutiny or on the other side, whimsically, due to personality divisions or seductive unholy favors asked or granted, to advance something. This adds another layer of extraneous frosting to the conflict of a significant business decision. Conflict then becomes something to avoid. It leads me to think that we must be honest with our true expectations by demanding more of management than cowering behind business relationships that are one sided, easy to please, and protecting interests. This forms a muted power alliance that potentially demeans sales representatives, clients and the company's goals to grow business.

An example I use is from when I worked on an idea to upgrade the advertising investment of a regional real estate company with a global footprint. My first point of contact was their agency, which showed no interest in the program, deeming it too hard to execute. Admittedly, it required effort. I didn't stop there, as I knew the client, albeit only casually. She was the national marketing director, a very can-do, dynamic individual who happened to love creative ideas. I explained the background of my discussions with her agency to her. She made a call to verify what I told her. Later in the week, she called me and said she would proceed without her agency. After six months of working closely with the client and her team, the campaign was visibly and monetarily successful. The client's agency then wanted a piece of the action. They met with my station manager and demanded an agency fee, threatening to pull their other clients off the air if they didn't receive it. I informed the client about this meeting and how my commissions would have been impacted, and she understood this. I recall her heels *thundering* down the hallway floor. She threatened to fire her agency unless they backed off and apologized. The agency sheepishly reversed their threats and backed off. Unfortunately, the general manager at our TV station had been ready to capitulate for fear of losing business. In his mind the client was never a consideration, although they had the real power. My relationship with this client flourished and it provided me with almost equal power to her agency, and besides that it was genuinely a good concept. The client recognized this, but the agency seemed only interested in maintaining the *status quo*. Eventually, she did fire this agency for their lazy thinking.

It has been said that there is no such thing as a bad or good decision. The good or bad is revealed only when the decision is actioned, and the results are tabled. The definition to me is just do something. Decide. Hoorah! You're either revered or jeered at. In some cases, both. The propositions unfold in your day-to-day sales life, tagging along as either a small or large decision; the good news is you are making choices that can either torpedo a sales proposition, or bring home the big catch from a fruitful day of fishing. All these uninvited decisions are based on either a methodical slow-burn substance or a shallow, fluffy marshmallow you can easily swallow.

Now, a decision can be simply characterized as a budget you're close to achieving, or a budget you haven't made in months. The conflict is internal and understandably selfish if you're strictly on commission. The process at first is *ad hoc* and informal as you introduce yourself to the shallow you. As you walk and laugh yourself away from the mirror. Confident self-talk can be a stunning introduction to the ease by which you perceive a problem. You think to yourself, "This issue can be easily resolved. I know the decision-makers, and they like me. Last week we had lunch. I'm covered. They like me." You repeat this chant *ad nauseam,* to yourself and others. Then something external unexpectedly happens that makes you question your entire professional existence and confidence.

"My best ally is leaving! I know the others, yes, but this person was the closest to me and the final decision-maker, and she really liked me a lot. We had a super relationship."

Another thought scrapes through your brain, "I think the other team members like me". The conflict that was once confident is now unfavorably modified into a humbling-mumbling philosopher, reading self-help business books with quotes from Marcus Aurelius. The process at that epiphanic point requires more realistic information. More thinking outside the books and more realignment by quickly learning who will replace this business friend. Enter Conscience 101 with tablet and Apple pen, asking probing questions inside the storm of your brain, tossing curiosity and debris all over your fragile self-esteem. It can bring you to your knees, clutching onto fear and an account that you may lose. You're thinking becomes bolder, "Will this affect their past strategy that included my product? Will this new person consider my product relevant, does this stranger like someone better, other than me? Maybe one of my other inferior associates? Is the current team, who happens to like me, able to push my proposal across the line? I did have a lunch with them that I was told they loved, and I gave them a bag of our company's logo goodies. They said the food was great, and they liked all the goodies. I'm sure they like me. I was voted best radio sales rep by their agency five years ago. Yeah, but the winning vote left the company. I'm alone! I'm abandoned! I'm fucked!"

Here's a suggestion that you may find useful before you have a mental breakdown: it is better to spread your influence on all decision-makers in whatever capacity they hold before it causes you to fold or seek a spiritual life. Instead of forming a relationship with one or two people that you happen to share an astrological sign with, it would be wise that all those who manage the business were on board your friendship cruise ship. Otherwise, when that one important person leaves, you'll be stuck with a painful self-evaluation, hoping that everyone likes you. This conflict is not an imaginary phantom rising from a bad-hair day. It is real, the circumspection of an awkward situation and thus cannot be underestimated. You can ponder if they like you or not, though that is more suited to a smiling social media emoji than a sober established trader of advertising time. The good news is you wouldn't have to be in martyred, self-inflicted agony if you had properly laid the basic groundwork with the entire team and they understood your product's value, as opposed to just making a good deal or enjoying a fun lunch. At each juncture, you have no choice but to dig in deeper and determine what the client captured, or didn't, regarding the benefits of your product, its position in the market and how it fits. If you spend a fair amount of time selling, as opposed to *schmoozing*, you won't have to worry about "like vs resource". You will see that your proposition is not compromised by one, or multiple, personnel shifts. You sold the product, not air-kisses. Your business will remain essentially alive in the vendor's eyes and there will be no pause button. The bonus is, you'll never worry sick if you're the most popular person in that agency again. You may even be honored with another reward. A reward for Team Facilitator. If a new client hire is inevitable, you should feel confident that your sphere of influence will spread to the other team members you already know, and the conflict resolution is that the new hire will like you, and you won't have to start building a relationship from ground zero. I learned this the hard way.

A major manufacturer in the food and beverage sector, one of the largest in the world, faced a significant corporate public relations issue. During my time working in print media, I developed a strong relationship with the product manager of their recipe and cheese division. We both identified that my product and her messaging were ideally suited for recipes and general health information. My rapport with her agency was robust and trustworthy, and they fully supported the use of my medium, encouraging direct communication with their client. After nearly a year of focusing on this product category and developing advertorial ideas, I was on the brink of closing the deal. As a reminder, this was a major company with an array of retail supermarket products, including corporate communications. Her influence within the company was significant, leveraging it would have given me access to other product managers. It was a retail opportunity for an ambitious media sales representative. However, it was Thanksgiving and, metaphorically, I was the turkey – too myopic and focused solely on one product, oblivious to the broader company portfolio. A few weeks later, the agency called, agreeing to proceed with my proposal, with the client's support. We celebrated the news over lunch, in a happy triumphant mood. A few days passed and I met with the client for lunch, just two weeks before Christmas. We toasted to the occasion and the hard work that had been invested. This was a prime example of a collaborative partnership with a client that moved beyond typical one-dimensional agency relationships. During our lunch, she assured me she would finalize the booking in January, post-holidays. Noticing my concerned expression, she inquired if something was wrong. Despite having no rational reason, a dark and deep-seated doubt persisted that this deal might never materialize, even though it seemed to be a slam-dunk, which both she and her agency had approved. I forced a smile for the balance of the lunch but remained uneasy. We didn't speak again until January. Whatever you want to call it, intuition or premonition, inside I felt uncomfortable for a long three weeks with what I was certain was only an insecure feeling. When I returned to work from the Christmas holiday, I received an urgent phone call from my client. Her voice was repentant. In my gut I knew where this conversation was heading, and it was right into a brick wall. She said the deal was dead. Corporate had a public relations calamity to avert. All advertising dollars within the company were being used to shape public perceptions and they would use the dollars on several different mediums, but not mine. It was too late to build any type of relationship when the company was forced to control a narrative in environments they were familiar with. My client had to throw her budget into the corporate hat. Even a sure thing could randomly be left in a pile of unpredictability. The best way to protect your business is finding the time to meet others within the company, who may not be directly involved now, but might be in the future. You must open and broaden your network to many different actors who work within a company or agency that you're courting. I learned that certainty is not a common yardstick to reach a definitive conclusion or truth. It is better to embrace uncertainty, and to remain flexible and curious. It's also better to talk to everyone and anyone that could use your services.

CHAPTER 28

Okay, client relationships. Again.

We need seriously reflect upon the ubiquitous virtual meeting. We need to scrap it where and when we can. First, let's continue our talk about customer relations. We should understand that there is no typical client/customer personality type.

Clients are delightfully unalike: flexible, irrational, sometimes too smart, sometimes too stupid, open, closed, young, middle-aged, old, male, female, trans, gay, straight, conservative, progressive, dismissive, positive, negative, Pisces, Capricorn, playful, serious, critical, flighty, mindful, forgetful, influenced, influencer, loner, party animal, direct, evasive, daffy, sane, pathological, thinking, feeling, adaptable, judging, appropriate, inappropriate, screamer, whisperer, arrogant, humble, vain, philosophical, plays too much golf, drinks and eats too much. The contrasts are endless.

In today's high-pressure environment, with the uncertainty of whom you'll be interacting with, you're likely to encounter the various personality types I mentioned. Volatility, in general terms, is another attribute in a businessperson conditioned to respond strategically, and they will be guided by their internal clock on who to meet or avoid. Titles often play a crucial role in this process, and even individuals with significant authority, such as kings or queens, may exhibit *prima donna* tendencies.

The person who sits directly in front of you during a meeting is never the same person who sits comfortably in their office, away from the pressures of making decisions. Therefore, understanding the complexity of human behavior should be foundational for further upskilling in sales. This critical understanding will enhance your negotiation abilities and bring balance to conversations.

What do I mean by balance? The seller and the buyer are generally at opposite ends. Interests may be similar, they both have needs, but each have different ways of achieving them. At your first meeting, introductions may be awkward and flimsy. The seller's goal is to sell something, while the buyer's initial reaction is naturally one of skepticism, and the impulse to push back, depending on how familiar you both are. How well they "dance" depends on one leading with confidence and flair while the other adeptly follows. Balance requires moves that blend to a *simpatico* union, where the conversation projects interest and openness. The dance underscores the balance of give-and-take in negotiations.

Everyone wants to achieve a harmonious interaction that leads to both parties receiving a beneficial outcome. The negotiations begin exactly at the point you meet the first-time prospect or when introducing a proposition to a chummy buyer. The dynamics are subtle in the initial meeting. You need to read and respond to social cues even before you dive into your presentation. It begins by assessing the person you are speaking with and the probability that this person will purchase something from you. You may place your faith in CRMs or ROIs, or the predictive patterns of past behavior of many in our industry. Data is everywhere! Everyone, including your competitors, have a stack of statistical justifications to convince, persuade and confuse a cynical jury.

Now, with the ever increasing disconnect between customer and sales executive, due to internal and external factors that aren't fitting the true narrative of selling (like the A-Z best seller sales manual you have tucked away somewhere), it serves as a sharp reminder that sales executives are operating by rote and employing archaic company practices. We bend over willfully to the impulse of narrow-thinking management and narrow-account fishing in a narrow creek or a narrow, closed market. The closed market exemplifies a rigid order of who you're allowed to see from your transferable client list—determining your movements and income.

In meeting after meeting, the end game is always to squeeze the product into a tight fist by dominating and smashing the entrepreneurial spirit. The creed is to sell anything; promote discounting and giveaways for whatever it takes to win. In the environment of product infertility there are winners and losers. Most of the losers loiter on the selling side. Why? The client has the power to say "no". That is a persuasive argument that needs no explanation.

Now, because of unforeseen events, many companies and their employees are in a foxhole. Present and future decisions are ill-advised when money is boxed in. Companies release key staff or compromise valuable business relationships to cover debt, and to cover for safety, using corporate hypotheses as evidence for their uncertain choices. Unprecedented events like pandemics, war and partisan politics have trapped companies and individuals in a cycle of riskiness, impairing what was once clear decision making. Working blindly, without a modern historical reference guide during these precarious times.

A new era for the "back-to-human" side of business is the correction that will bring growth and assurance. Its facility has the expanse to shape an original business model using fragments from the past, like consultation, that will materialize results. The one thing that is perennial, and that remains within us, is our human connection and spirit. The essential elements overshadowed by our reliance and awe of technology are like believing that pressing a laptop keyboard harder will invoke blessings from saints and demigods. As our technological dependence increases, it threatens our workforce by shrinking their ability to "think" and to "act". This leads to a base of stagnancy and procrastination that ultimately slows or shuts down the activity of deliberation. We need to foster a balance between technology, as an obvious tool, and the crucial elements of critical thinking and proactive behavior.

Any information or impressions delivered slovenly over a virtual meeting are diluted; like drowning premium whiskey with water, it will lack the potency and intensity of an aged whiskey that has reached maturity. Similarly, too much structure can breed inactivity. We need to imagine a new future forward in sales. A future that retools the personal sales branding away from passive interactivity. A new, expressive future of community, sharing and persuasion, leading us away from passive observation and online interaction. Auto-generated data creates a simulated conversation, replacing real people and the extension of thought, debate and real-life situations. The eager algorithm lab mice are wearing the white coats, and we are sitting in mix-matched cages waiting to be augmented. The truth is, there isn't really a one-size-fits-all, typical client or meeting. There are patterns of behavior, yes, and that may seem the same or easily definable, but the human mind with all its strength and imagination is still flaccid, emotional and easily swayed by perceptions that are borrowed or bought.

The most valuable currency we have in sales is client relationships that are manifested. Despite this, we inadvertently allow faceless computer algorithms to intrude, diverting the possibility of a frank and personal encounter. We trust technology more than ourselves, often accepting half-truths, and swapping constructive conversations (we're always in a hurry) and thorough research for what is ultimately speed and convenience. The most meaningful interaction between a sales representative and a client is the irreplaceable connection forged through human contact. Therefore, make it your mission to get that meeting with the client. If you don't, someone else will.

Business AI technology has its function as a support servant and could open your mind to many other possibilities and mechanisms in dissecting and distilling information. But you must open your eyes to its limitations.

In our partially sealed world of what we receive and generate, human connectivity is far more indispensable today than ever before. The global pandemic and post-pandemic have left us drumming and wandering in and out of our computer screens, like a marching band routinely going up and down the same street, hour by hour, not knowing the next steps to success.

If your company's sales culture is heavily reliant on dull administrative technology that closes one eye to minimal client meetings, your negotiations will be severely limited and untapped. Your personality will be like a basset hound jogging. Your sales numbers will forever be unpredictable and mostly forgettable. Today, businesses should run like a wombat to avoid being run over with consultants and their fancy charts, leading to a non-solution. If you are in sales or dream about joining this elite group of professionals, open your aptitude by not attaching powerlessness to your potential or vision.

Beware of the social media gathering that blatantly encourages sameness, skewing bad habits unreservedly. It will only alter you as it has anonymous others.

The blog or podcast you watch or listen to is more added noise from voices that are crying for attention. Be discerning with what you allow into your head space. Otherwise, you're left shapeless, inauthentic and questioning your right to own a Land Rover. Ask yourself, how many personal real-life stories of personal suffering and mendacious propaganda can the mind take? Will we return to normal? Unlikely.

Clients promote their product in social media to influence and engage new customers. Maybe you can return the serve by showering, getting dressed and showing up at the office. This is the first step towards a genuine business alliance with you and your commitment. You can hide – and of course, many do – by playing hide-and-seek with the latest technology, a rude plague or grinning apes banging bongo sticks; hiding is convenient when you don't want to disturb the universe or participate in the moment. The real story is about accountability with your job and you. Let's face it, people actually do prefer a real signature over a click, a real coffee over a virtual one and a real person over a doll.

Be brave, and memorably unpredictable, in the vibrant meeting places or traverse solitary in the digital highway that is crowded and at a stand-still.

CHAPTER 29

Clients hide.
Agencies police the corridors of power.

A common complaint I hear from sales reps is how difficult it is to get an appointment with a client. Much of what I discuss in this book relates to client appointments and their significance in closing business deals. I know there are sales reps who meet with clients every day. I often see them at posh restaurants, sipping pinot and enjoying fusion dishes. Yet, for most sales reps, getting a one-on-one with a client is harder than getting one with the Dalai Lama (excuse the pun). Why is there is such a chasm between sales reps and clients? Some blame social media and new technology. In media, some blame paranoid, controlling agencies. For example, when a rep tries to contact a client, they might be given an impersonal email starting with "info@", you may well have been sent to outback Australia, where you will wander underground for the rest of your career.

New technologies are gatekeepers, now working in unison with human ones. It's true that in today's sales environment it is very challenging to secure appointments. It does depend on the industry you are in, and market conditions that allow or don't allow freer expression. One realistic reason that clients avoid sales reps is the oversaturation of outreach attempts by many sales reps, clamoring for the client's attention. That is the reason you must stand out in a positive way. Of course, technology has complicated the human experience with impersonal communication devices, so they create barriers like generic email addresses to send everyone to the same place. In saying that, digital tools also provide unprecedented access to decision-makers with greater visualization of data analytics and smarter business efficiency. To connect the 20th century to the 21st successfully, it's important to adapt to the evolving business landscape. As digital dominates more of clients' time, using programmatic advertising for example, it is reducing the need for direct human interaction. Additionally, hiring discounting agents to sell "unsold inventory" adds another layer to your strategy. However, this approach sometimes inadvertently competes with real sales representatives who work hard to secure value through their rates. While desperate rate-cutting might initially seem beneficial, it's not a sustainable future for building your company's fortunes.

There are companies that use novel, and deliciously extravagant, methods to meet new clients. This brands them as players in a market that fluently spends more money, spilling excesses to win favor and influence. They invite important clients to a private party right out of a Netflix movie, with sumptuous designer-chef food, top shelf drinks and loud ABBA music (okay, it's not Afrobeats) but, boy oh boy, the expensive corporate packaging with big tit blue and white balloons is a spectacle you'll never forget. Move out of the way, tech-heads, and welcome human connection with a capital C! The eye-watering-priced penthouse with a 360-degree killer view of Sydney Harbour, is enough to make you feel like the royal family. The most jaded of titans are taking selfies, laughing and smiling with their big, crowned teeth to show the world and their connections that they are the chosen ones. Later they'll share it on social media to the drooling wannabees. The elite is hard at work.

The proud chieftain of the host company guides a small number of people to a private presentation room for intimacy and an intoxicated sell. A drink in their hand, the titans are devoured by a room decorated in cash and splendor. The 8K screen preserves the integrity of technological advancement while redeeming the extraordinary outlay and effort to indoctrinate new followers. The chieftain displays the company's latest and greatest product, its wow features and, of course, wealth. After the orgasmic viewing, the mesmerized group is sent back out to the multicentre drinking room; the pouring, pounding rain-lights and tribal dancing, along with the ABBA soundtrack, are like the veins of the elderly, ungainly and thick with youth possession. In comes the next group for indoctrination with Sir Wow leading the stupor party, a replay of a 10- or 15-minute video projecting the future of advertising on a unique billboard platform that is integrated with sky, clouds and perturbed birds.

The black-tie luxury of this event goes on all night, and some stay even longer into the early morning. Raindrops glitter, French champagne flows and the loftiest of seafood and loud happy-to-be-here conversation shakes like Jerry Lee Lewis from floor to ceiling. The evening is special. It must be. Everyone that was influential showed up and probably spent hours at home deciding on their wearables for this media proposition—I mean *party*. When you walk in the white polished, sterile expansive room, you can't help but be impressed, as you're greeted by a smart tuxedoed staff member offering the ubiquitous champagne, red and white wines, or beer. Move a few feet into the room and the drinks and seduction are cascading all over you, ready to be grabbed and swallowed like a homeless Thanksgiving meal. I don't know when sales became an event, or an incongruous soundtrack, but one thing is for sure: the client-meeting backlash has softened. Companies must push forward with creative ways of introducing their product to clients, even if it is over the top. In this example, the sales rep had the CEO's support and a pricey investment in getting the client to their table, or dancing on it. These are sales tools to open closed doors and invite the sales reps to sit at the table. Media sales representatives are fast becoming fragmented in a field of sameness, from a hungover industry with too many laps to the wine table, who rely on heavy relationship selling. More needs to be done by hands-on managers to realize their real role within the company. It's not to spit out data for vernacular GMs but to be the gate opener for the sales team.

Clients and their agencies have radically departed from the old school of one-representation selling, but they don't know it yet. They're still too busy playing the short-sighted game of one-person-comfort representation. It takes an entire company with communicable ideas to replace the wholesale discounting by a solitary rep that will leave your product faceless; it is no longer sufficient to have a one-dimensional selling strategy. The shared client solution from harried managers commonly rears its head because two reps tripped over each other by each covering their client's business, but both not wholly identifying all the significant players. Then management assigns the agency and the client to two reps. To the manager, which rep has the strongest influence on this business is unclear. One client is then assigned to both. The client finishes last. Becoming an adjunct to the wider scope of a business arrangement both internally and externally. It creates unnecessary pressures about fairness, with the external limitations of a sales executive to manage the business to completion, the dichotomy of a sales executive understanding both the client and the agency and the dependence of others' activity. All of this plus trusting their selling skills and leaving tenure to chance and another rep who may not have your ability to sell. Inevitably the lack of real accountability plays a major role. The buyers keep on getting jaded and controlling for no apparent reason except "I like this sales rep, and I don't need to have another rep". These people can walk, swim and socialize on the internet but having one more rep paralyzes them. The unfortunate "connect-the-dots" sales manager is generally left with an interpersonal mess. A mess that has nothing to do with selling, but everything to do with partiality. It introduces two conflicts where nothing is fully accomplished or resolved. The agency – or *daycare* –allows a patronage that is biased. Aided by the manager, who is carried away by either an agitated client or likely an agency. The two reps in the background delegating fear of a rookie representation onto their business partner. "They like only me"—which has replaced the fable question "mirror, mirror on the wall…"

In my experience sales executives work smarter and harder when they are allowed to complete a task without interference or being micro-managed, stereotyped and segregated. It's the way for all industries and humans. Reliance on strict enforcement and sanctions is the death knell of a company. If the company's rules prevent a sales rep from following the money and fulfilling the arrangement with the client, it is simply a political rampart that will prevent the ease of business through steady continuity with the destination. Rules that usurp good business practices are puzzling, but it is mundanely common. After all, business is meant to be fearless, not tied to a weak bridge that eventually, in a short time, collapses. I've seen it time and time again how questionable rules allow a company culture to degrade the process and fade into mediocrity. Rules vs client's interest is plain stupid, especially if the rules are dictated by a third party or the client. When is the local manager useful and bringing value to their title? When an introduction is warranted for an assigned rep on an account. It's an endorsement, instead of attempting to discourage the open passage for their sales rep, or siding with an agency complaint of too many reps wandering around their building. Without introspection and proper sales support, it becomes a lazy solution to placate a lazy agency. It requires reinforcement, repetition and comfortable professionalism to believe in the flow of business. It takes finesse to defend your company's values and your sales rep's reputation. Don't throw your sales rep under the bus to gain superhero status by winning unwinnable favors. If you want to be seen as a comic book, get a shitload of tattoos instead and don't forget the steroids.

There could be an exciting sales future for businesses who smash the old fashion idea of territories traditionally designed to constrict reps and make them poorer. If the barriers no longer exist, business relationships will expand and move beyond a smallish inner circle of dubious favors. After all, the company and the sales rep will benefit. There should be no state franchises! No one ownership of an advertising agency. No Trump-like walls! No ownership of a market that neutralizes the sales rep and the company's profitability! The business of sales must be consistent and confident so that each member of a team is trained in excellence and is able to sit at any table, in any network, in an open, buoyant marketplace.

These days, we can effortlessly connect across the globe. However, many companies remain entrenched in outdated company cultures that prioritize conformity over innovation. This stifling environment often leads to exaggerated friendships, and superficial movements that prevent the development of essential skills and impact financial performance. A marketplace that suffocates fresh ideas, encourages missed opportunities, as promising sales teams are held back. The ability to control the market and not to be controlled is paved with unexpected benefits if the plan is executed with careful thought by grasping the nuances of the market and human behavior. Too many naysayers in a company will defeat progress and opportunity. If you have a product that delivers results, the tools you need should be simple, straightforward and rewarded. It is that unscripted momentum that will help to overcome doubt and push business deals away from your competitor, structured robotically to follow an old script. Ownership is an ego entitlement and control, whether it's by a title or a legacy, is the birthing place for complacency. A fast-starting, ambitious sales rep with no geographical boundaries will have more than enough gas or petrol to overtake defeat. Business relationships, like personal relationships, allow choice-slippage with a dogmatic mindset based on a small network of friends and social business acquaintances. It's called nepotism or incest. It's not a good thing. Sales representatives don't intentionally lose business; they are products of their manager's direction, whether it is brave or cautious, progressive or outdated. Today's sell-structure is heavily biased to failure in a viciously repetitive environment. The current sales strategies are poorly designed or simply ineffective, leading to repeated copycat failure. Attempts to succeed keep meeting with the same negative outcome.

An updated and modern sales structure, incorporating ongoing training, will create a dynamic framework, fostering individualistic thinking by expanding accessibility and reducing movement restrictions. Adhering to an outdated model that provides illusory convenience wrapped in mediocrity ensures the refrain of "it's a hard market" will remain persistent. Instead, allow the sales rep to follow the money to wherever that destination may be. I've met many managers who truly believe their market is different or special: Rio vs Sydney vs Nashville for example. Physically they are different, the way they speak and their food pleasure offerings, (though American fast-food chains have ruined a lot of the local variety), but it still proves my theory of similarities between food and business.

I've been fortunate to work globally for the past 20 years, experiencing the rich, embodied cultures of both the wealthy and the poor. Through this journey, I've realised that, fundamentally, we are all the same. In sales the buying objections were similar. The media platform I presented was similar. The client/agency media language was similar. Client power or agency control of the client was similar. Whether it was in English-speaking or non-English-speaking countries, the sales game was, unsurprisingly to me, similar. Even with distinct cultural and language differences, nothing had articulated a redesign or electronic head translation. In countries that don't speak your language, if you have a qualified translator that understands the language of your industry, you're hitting home runs and cutting through the communication barriers. I learned there is more value in understanding and respecting the culture you're navigating, than knowing the correct pronunciation of *konnichiwa*. Some senior managers, including multilingual ones, visiting overseas displayed an ethnocentric attitude toward the locals, which was divisive, hurtful and arrogant. Their ignorance led to suspicion and a breakdown in communication. The product may have had no obvious change or acknowledged advancement by an individual, but the product was ransomed or stagnated just from a too-familiar connection and friendship to keep the peace and enjoy the meal. Granted there are privileges in having an airtight client/sales rep relationship. But if the friendship is too tightly fitted, the friendship or familiar appendage is valued more than receiving the spoils of hard selling, negotiations and recursive results. It's a high wire act that needs discipline to find balance, and it begins with self-awareness, detachment and courage training.

I spent many years working in Brazil, but my skills in Portuguese were limited to greetings, and a rudimentary level of understanding. There was never an electronic accompaniment to me or the translator. It was much better 'singing *a cappella*' with my translator. If I were talking too fast, or there was something I said that she couldn't transcribe, I would get a gentle kick under the table. We purposely arranged to sit close to each other to assist this synchronicity and comprehension. The gentle kick was my cue to stop talking and address her concern. We would have a quick *tete-a-tete* and continue as if nothing had happened. The goals in my selling narrative were always focused on the client and their company. Too many "forks and knives" along the road may hinder your journey if you're distracted by inflated budgets and outdated policies that are more personal than they are proficient. Listen to the world's heartbeat as you travel through its blood. The pulse of friendships is in curio shops or over a glass of wine or *cachaca* in a neighborhood bar. Remove the lens of hegemony—travel light, open and side by side with strangers.

CHAPTER 30

Sales reps we all know.

The varied personalities of sales representatives are truly astonishing. Some seek guidance throughout their careers, holding hands with their managers as if on a quaint picnic, carving metaphorical hearts on bored trees. Others resemble government workers, meticulous administrators, who perfect spreadsheets with awe-inspiring technical precision. Then there are those marked by an elevated sales logic characterized by curiosity and persistence. They spend their days asking probing questions and pushing their agendas to the point where even an Olympic weightlifter would succumb. They blend tenacity with strategic facts, creating a cocktail of high drive and almost ruthless persuasion. In certain circles they might even be considered modern day philosophers on the move, proselytizing to knowledge-seeking peers by offering comfort and an honest examination of a client or company policy.

Each type of sales representative brings unique strengths to a team. Emphasizing these diverse skills and merging them effectively will create a powerful sales force. The key for managers is to recognize and cultivate these traits to align with the overall sales goals. You do not want a team of clones whose only strength is mundane sameness. Managers tend to mirror themselves with new hires they pick and reject the business of what individuals can bring to a company. A sales team is like a multicultural society, with all different types of people adding color and depth to the streetscape. Within the coming and going of movement in trade there are, in my experience, three types that stand out. Although there are elements of each of these individuals in most salespeople I examine below, these types are exclusively locked and dominated by a built-in structure overriding instincts, direction or instruction.

THE SUPERSTAR:

There's one in every sales team. The one whose ability goes beyond the norm that is expected. This almost unnaturally driven person is polarizing to both peers and management. They bring in a substantial amount of revenue that impacts positively on a company's growth and market status. They are alternately admired and reviled. Admired for their enormous and consistent results and reviled for their arrogance, corruptibility and Machiavellian values. Superstar sales reps create a whirlwind of revenue and gossip wherever they go, sharing secrets and insights with those they trust, until trust is gone. They often disregard company policies and see all competition as mere hurdles to overcome. Principles are just another game piece to them. They exude a blend of wild confidence and unpredictability, often appearing amazingly assured accompanied by an intriguing amount of unhinged. Their actions within the company can be as treacherous as the historical betrayal of Cassius against Marcus Aurelius in ancient Rome—a complex tale that has become a cautionary one in history. These overachievers are odd, with work routines often steeped in cunning plans, unexpected tactics and relentless selling. Despite their unusual methods, and in between the treachery, they are busy bringing in plenty of *moolah* to make the company's top brass overlook the bad parts. What's a few casualties for one big money-making, destructive machine helping to keep us afloat? The patience will last until one or two top *honchos* get their pants singed. Then things around the corral get interesting. This is a conflict with no obvious resolution. The big reflection in the manager's mind is to either fire this person immediately and risk the company's profits or bring in a brave lion tamer. The lion tamer option at the start sounds sensible, that is, until the lion tamer loses its whip, its chair and its head. I am not saying that all superstar sales reps aren't capable of real friendship, acts of kindness or saintly aspirations like the sainted Mother Teresa, but I haven't met one.

Many superstar reps have a killer "take-no-prisoner" instinct, but in fairness, they may question their mortality from time to time with an internal punch-up between greed and asceticism. A neurotic, serial seller of dubious ethics constantly in conflict with admirable drive and artfully running over peers. Without any barriers they are unstoppable in generating revenue, always walking on the edge of self-importance, while slightly evolving to a demigod status, without ever getting there. They'll seduce or reduce anyone who gets in their way. For them it is no longer about making a good income or even a life changing income. They wander in the negative "ego" territory needing to be number one. The number one son! The number one daughter! The number one biller! Number one in the eyes of the CEO and managers! The number one sales rep that clients love, or often equally loathe as well. This is the diabolical side to their success, the indescribable, disturbing restlessness driving them to prove to all that they are worthy, that they are unbeatable and that they should be feared and admired. And if they aren't feared, vengeance will rule and civilization as we know it will end. When they breathe, turn away, as the bubble of a world ending will navigate like a swollen river violently into your drowning mouth. You should only have one in your sales team, if you can afford to hire a good shrink to keep that person busy with themselves and away from mankind.

I'D RATHER TALK TO A SCREEN:

These types are the strangest of reps. One foot in sales while the other two feet are under a desk. They are a freakish lot. I would label as crazy any sales reps who believe the best motto in selling is DO NOT DISTURB. That is, you shouldn't own a human voice. Everything is done via email or social media, and all communication is best on an impersonal and distant scale. Internet stalking is their sales strategy. They are generally older in age and stuck in a stagnant yesteryear comfort zone. Occasionally they will find luck and get bite-sized sales here and there, but mostly their self-preserved cave is not the best environment to build relationships. It has far too many limitations with which to express growth and success. It's close to being a psychological disorder like the superstar with borderline insecurity. Let's face it, sales is a scary business—pile upon pile of rejections on all levels from respected industry people. You could easily become a mass murderer from all the rejection. The "talk to the screen" sales rep is so far removed from the selling experience that it leans toward solely being an administrative activity. This person can be very convincing to managers and some peers with their in-depth knowledge of data, graphs and an opinionated critical market assessment. The bury-my-head-in-the-screen sales rep will confide that they don't work very well with other people, either in-house or on the street. They are not as flamboyant or popular as the extroverted sales reps who constantly entertain clients and write business almost daily as a sideline. The sales rep who prefers conversing with a screen tends to be highly judgemental of their peers and managers. They often compare what they perceive as their superior intellectual ability to analyze research and numbers more efficiently to their perceived slower-witted counterparts, who must endure endless, tedious in-person meetings.

Sometimes their superiority is amplified as they announce a slapstick version of a research project that no one understands. They love a good information camouflage that makes them look more astute than a popular blogger. It becomes pointless, this non-selling, and it does not serve the company well. This type of sales rep is faithful to a dogmatic style of "selling" by believing it's the most effective way to bring in customers, partly because of a social awkwardness enhanced by unwholesome computer engagement.

However, they do have merit, by offering a comprehensive strategic picture of sales competence. If only they would add a higher level of external enthusiasm and be sighted in the marketplace a little more frequently than Bigfoot. There is justification for this type of sales individual. The blend of science and personality would be formidable. Unfortunately, this type of sales rep falls short of attaining consistent or effective level selling standards. They are disconnected to the emotional side of selling. Their disconnection with real people speaks volumes about their fears of rejection and failure. They are difficult to manage and train with an opinion of themselves as superior.

In time, they morph into uninteresting, highly dependent office furniture. They are defensive and opinionated. A strange and useless combination of sales loathing and delusion, believing they are the cornerstone of account management. They are not sales reps. They are imposters in need of a title— in either administration or sales support.

THE ACE IN YOUR TEAM:

This person does everything by the book. In fact, they do it from the many books they read to increase their sales skills.

Also, from what they learned from their sales history, working in other companies, and keeping up with current up-to-date sales tips and tricks from bloggers, podcasts and associates. They are eager to learn and will store this knowledge for quick access as a diverse mental sales library when needed. They have an expanding toolbox, where they find the best utility for the right moment. They are keen observers as they plan their day and week. They are discerning and will work with management or other parts of the company, to skillfully navigate the best option to close a deal. And they worry. They worry about every small detail of the sales process. This worry brings a needy anxiety, to ensure that all communication is covered, whether they are proposals, or even friendly negotiations. It always never is.

Nevertheless, they will always, and I mean always, go far above the expected to help a client with anything they ask for, or information that may or may not be relatable or required, to get closure. Whereas the Superstar rep will do almost anything in their power to avoid client requests as they see it as client trivialities, the Ace in your team has bundles of enthusiasm and confidence creating a can-do environment wherever there is opportunity, while doing everything to reduce the "chance" part of selling.

Another major benefit in having an Ace in your staff is that they motivate the other reps on the team. Some may adopt that person as a mentor or a close friend. They may not mirror the Ace's zeal and precision, but the rub-off effect on the others will have measured results from all the players on the team. The Ace on your team is not a loyal employee to one person. They are too pragmatic for that! They will work under several mentors or managers if they believe there is a conjoint of ideas and objectives. Their sole purpose is to sell and make money—as any successful sales rep should. They have a unique understanding of the importance of continuous sales training and importing fresh ideas. That's one solid reason why they're frequently one of the top producers. They are curious and ego free, an important aspect of all human relationships that rely on daily business interaction.

This type of all-rounder rep is a breath of fresh air for any manager who is feverishly driving sales and chasing impossible budgets. They are not interested in office small talk, (most of the time) or sharing their personal life to associates. They come to work to work. They rarely waste time on a screen looking at social media. They don't spend time in the office kitchenette. They're too busy channelling clients to worry about pursuing "likes" on social media. They are competitive and they will "scoreboard" the other reps, to not only see their stats but, more importantly, see where their associates sit on pricing, client size and the tracking of future business. Like the Superstar rep they relish being number one, but they don't mean harm to others. You will not be character assassinated by an Ace if their numbers are not at the top of the ranking. But they will continue to climb harder up that slippery tree.

They love to role-play, enacting client sales interchanges, with aplomb and gusto. They take the game seriously, as if they are auditioning for a Scorsese film. The Ace will stay in character and bring so much animation and aptitude that it becomes compelling live theatre. Yet with all these wonderful attributes, be on guard if a manager or associate critiques a fault in their role-play. They will fold their arms and sulk, quietly disappearing among the perceived negative exchange from the participators. In the next role-play they'll come even better prepared; like a missing limb that regenerates itself, there is regrowth in their activity. At times, they can be hypercritical of their associates for the smallest display of incompetence. Questioning their motives by tossing around conspiracy theories off a paranoid page from Spokane militia men. Quickly they return to business, and no one gets executed.

In my experience, I would identify them as the closest to being the quintessential sales rep. Generally well-groomed, even when the office is liberal in casual dress policies, they are polished and claim they want to be dress-ready for any random meeting that, well, rarely happens. In an office of jeans, T-shirts and sneakers, they are emblematic of a time in the days long ago where empowerment of perceptions favored stability and trust. Always reliable and a pleasure to work with, they'll keep management on their toes with plenty of questions and what they perceive as fair or unfair from company management. Fearless and aloof.

CHAPTER 31

Grinning apes picking fleas.

The "ballerina" sales rep effortlessly pirouettes and leaps into perfect precision form whenever the marketing department supplies them with company logos, cupcakes or custom-logo calendars. There's cherry logo jam, logo gift grab bags, logo polo shirts, logo pens, logo USB drives, logo umbrellas, logo yoga mats and logo phone chargers, all emblazoned with logos everywhere. It's astounding the lengths to which companies will go to be memorable and persuasive in the eyes of their client. The marketing team constantly unveils the latest gimmicks to saturate the market and earn applause. If the brand remains omnipresent and recognized, these contrived freebies serve a purpose. Here is a scene that is not so far from reality:

Sales Manager to Sales Rep: "Who are you seeing today?"

Sales Rep to Sales Manager: "Busy week! I have to drop off all these cupcakes to the agencies."

LATER IN THE DAY

Sales Manager to GM: "A big week for the reps. This cupcake promotion really works; the agencies love it!"

GM to Sales Manager: "Next time, let's have a national bowling party for clients. We can give away cash prizes for the winners, and an all-expense trip to Bali for the entire winning agency."

Sales Manager to GM "Great idea! Love it! They'll talk about it for the rest of their lives—brilliant idea! Clients love free trips!"

GM to Sales Manager: "How do we track the results? It will be awfully expensive. I'll have to justify it to the board, even though I handpicked most of them."

Sales Manager to GM: "No problem. We can marry our online social media to the clients LinkedIn accounts with pictures of Bali and our logo. Can you imagine the "likes" and comments that will be pouring in. Remember the fish research we presented to our clients and agencies? Whether a fish had the ability to understand simple hand sign commands better than the deaf? They bought it: Hook, line, and sinker! (*They both laugh.*)

GM to Sales Manager: I remember. Did we, uh, make any money? I do recall handing out swimming caps with our logo on it. Weren't they waterproof? My wife still wears it to bed (*wink*). I think I can get this one approved by her and the board (*they both laugh*).

Sales Manager to GM: We made money! Although It's hard to validate the actual numbers as some clients are on fixed annual contracts. The only other model I used for sourcing new business revenue is with our direct business sales team. I remember we picked up some local business. Like "The School of Finger and Thumbs-Up" the online sign language course. Our direct reps went gangbusters on the street.

GM to Sales Manager: Weren't they the people that wanted their ad read in sign language?

Sales Manager: Yes, we worked it out. I told them our radio audience prefer recorded ads.

Asymmetrical marketing often fails to achieve lasting success in the competitive quest to win customer loyalty. It tends to be fleeting and forgettable when all competitors indulge in grand promotions and extravagant events. I find it comical that grown people in an intelligent and can-do industry believe that an inferior or openly palm-greasing idea will bring positive, long-term revenue and add fidelity to their free-for-all business. It chimes with desperate, lazy thinking, ringing everywhere in the creative hallways of commerce. Sales teams are eager to seize any opportunity to engage and meet with clients, even if it means offering giveaways that demand nothing from the client except their presence. The only benefit comes from the opportunity for a meeting. These tactics all serve two purposes – client connection and client loyalty – even if it's only for that moment. In sales, recognition and noticeable incentives often go hand in hand. If we want our product to be remembered, quickly get your professional sales reps to sit at the negotiating table and leave the cupcakes in the oven. Lower the heat on the marketing gimmicks and confectionary. We must meticulously train our sales representatives in the art of selling, encompassing price negotiation skills and a deep understanding of human behavior. I'm not suggesting that the marketing team should be fired, but more perhaps turning their attention to the product's value. A different perspective or concept that will progress the sales reps' meetings to a fuller client experience. Sales reps are spending far too much time in the office or waiting for trivial company merchandise to accompany them to their meetings.

Chasing clients is like a three-legged rhino charging askew, spreading the dust of its shortcomings in clumsy ineptness and urgent aimlessness. If you're captive to a primitive work environment, run by remote straw men or overcooked ape personalities having very little business acumen, you may notice that when challenged, they will grunt and easily fold like a fake dollar or a closing umbrella.

The grinning apes look at sales training as soft and inconsequential. In all my years in sales, I've never encountered a sales rep properly trained in negotiation. When the cold wind of a stalemate sets in, it's no wonder the negotiation freezes. Some have read an occasional book on the principles or steps to follow, but nothing close to fundamental instructions. You will find that closing a sale will become soluble when your sales structure is based on trial and error. The more successful reps that have skills in networking and established relationships still fall short in negotiations if it requires conflict and discomfort. They chase yesterday's business and plan off past results. Sales results are only truly understood by deep-studying sales habits and training, the continuity of activity solely dependent on forward training methods instead of just experience, the product's brand, established friendships and luck—or a well-padded client list. The restructuring of sales priorities that invigorate fortified training is the foundation of sales stability. Managers who are steadfast and narrowly punctual to numbers, and not people, will view training as a waste of time. If they open their eyes to see how many staff are removed mechanically on a regular basis, they will clearly know the reason for their company's crippled culture and lack of reflexivity to produce an assertive sales team with assertive results. On going sales training is the tool sharpener of the mind, one that allows an evolution of thinking by enhancing the way you think, leading to better judgement and decision-making in business contexts. It underscores the importance of lifelong learning and skill improvement in making strategic business decisions.

CHAPTER 32

Your manager needs to keep busy.

When a sales manager rides or shadows a sales rep's client meeting for non-crucial appointments, they diminish the rep's credibility in the eyes of the client. There is also plenty of self-interest shown by a manager, who inevitably crows about the tryst and how their influence and accomplishments were essential at these meetings, to the upper echelon of the company. A sales manager can avoid the need for overreach by ensuring that they have a highly skilled sales team, and one that is independent of them, requiring minimal manager interference. If the business meeting is complex and the sales rep is inexperienced, then a joint call with the manager has validity and is encouraged. The significance of being too attached to your manager will either diminish or heighten your career. Therefore, you must be careful which side you want to be on. Your rise or fall will be dependent on you not plunging into a directive headfirst, because you believe you have no political choice. If you're as frequently in the manager's office as you are the coffee shop, it's because you want something handed over to you—either approval, or familiarity with your unfamiliar self (affirmation). Especially if that manager carries a juicy client list to offset your income. The singular attention you should seek is the discipline in client connectivity. This, and only this, will provide a rich alternative to ass-kissing and a prayer.

I went on many calls with sales teams in Brazil, Canada, Mozambique, The Gobi Desert, Moldova and the US. I advised the sales reps to only take me on calls that will help in making a difference. For example, high priority calls with senior clients or agencies were the given. I did not sell or pitch rates at these calls. That was the rep's responsibility. I was not there to take any of their credibility or clout away from them. The client must always know the rep is the go-to person. I wasn't at those meetings to be a hero (giving them everything they ask when the sales rep already clearly said no) or acting with bombastic self-importance. I helped the meetings by building blocks of colorful and interesting stories, by giving them a more deep-seated understanding of my product and my company's global footprint. I used it as an opportunity to define our shared and equal values. It was non-threatening to the client because it didn't require a decision or an execution. I didn't have to foreclose on one thought process to purchase another. It became an exchange that was not reserved or selective, but open to friendship. Later, the sales rep would follow my tracks and progress it to the next level. Each step you take should be another step forward. Consider your own life and a life choice you made that took you to a better place. There are always next steps in our lives. We don't stop and shut down on a clock. Each morning, we wake to the routine of our lives and the thunder in our heart. We spend some time eating. We spend some time in the bathroom. We spend some time making decisions. We spend some time exercising. We spend some time planning. We spend some time shopping. We spend some time with media. We spend some time with family and friends. We spend some time working. We don't stop. That is unless we're dead.

Every day you must familiarize yourself with the next steps to move forward—especially in the business of sales. When you finish a meeting with a client, ask them and yourself, "what's our next step?" Plan not just for today or whatever you can see. Visualize beyond that.

The visualization of the deal will help you close the deal. Try not to force the next step. Instead, make it as casual as a summer breeze but visualize it. Relationships in business are mainly built on reciprocity, trust and the frequency of your exposure to the client. There is generally disturbing chaos in making decisions outside of the norm. If the pattern in your business and personal life is unbalanced, with the occasional high but mainly lows, it's time for an assessment of whether you're following an unworkable pattern. Foresight is critical for any decision if the results you get are the same, year in, year out. In other words, just because an entire industry has been doing something the same way for years, doesn't mean you can't adapt, break new ground or determine a different way to ultimately reach your goal. There's always a war inside you, with every decision that is bold, different and considered. Be brave.

Following books that advise you to do it this way or that way, with a hundred action steps, is like looking for followers on Instagram without a *shtick* or a name. No one is interested in just seeing your face, except your mother. In a short time, your business will disappear, unless you can skillfully pickpocket favors from your manager.

Not everyone is built for sales, just as not everyone is built for marriage or a monastic life. I've met many bright and articulate people who "fell into" their sales career. It often happens as a fall-back career when they don't know what else to do. They'll give it an adequate try and within six months they're on their way to another job interview, testing their imagined ambitions with hopefully a punchier resume. Many return to sales after once again getting lost in that career orbit. They may blame their previous employer, their beat-up Kia or the lousy product they were forced to peddle. Whatever the reasons are, it's generally the divided self, the unconstructed self, that just can't fit or find the pieces that complete the whole.

The sales business is mentally gruelling. It is demanding and exceptionally hostile to many floundering sales reps. The distinguished and highly successful authors of self-help books that espouse "Managing Your Sales Like a Boss", "The A to Z of Super-Duper Sales Strategies" or "Life /Work Balance Naked on a Beach in Puerto Rico" speak to the mass consumers—and the mass gullible.

The new culture of sampling the latest trendsetting idea, op-eds, quick-fix modern adaptations of stoicism or the *Bhagavad Gita* all forfeit rectitude when it's all wrapped in *e-pop* talk. The relationship you may employ with ego-work is dull and short term. All you are asked to do is subscribe and share. As humans and computers merge and fornicate, we will see our work, ethics and communication skills chugging along in rudimentary speak, driven by a host of cutting-edge technological arrangements within the faster-than-blinking movement of the internet. It is already happening to us in our ordinary workday. An unbelievable number of companies allowing you to work from home, work from the beach, work from a café, work while shopping. I wonder why we call it work. The white robotic (not graceful) swan spinning on the fast-moving lake is where the uncertainty is taking us. Distancing us from personal experiences as our pointy heads face blinding screens and too much espresso. The deliberate forgotten face-to-face activity with clients is an example of corporate fusion supplanting a new order of non-assemblage and automated factory life on the go. Meanwhile we wander alone waiting, for the dog to blow the whistle.

There are brilliant minds who are designing and experimenting by combining the old with the new in the business of sales and client connection. Unfortunately, those who are mediocre will inevitably and demonstrably tip the axis of power towards an innocuously hand-picked mannequin that looks like a colony of wax ants, fully formed but devoid of life, without true purpose. The off-putting, freakish, moving parts with instructions are ready to propel us into our imagination. The manipulation of our gaze at something imagined is like revisiting a dream that has no timeline. We know something has toured our mind as we walk away from exploring this phantasm, but it's beyond indescribable. The microscopic observations enhance an institutional mindset ironed downed by childish disbelief and imagined poor performance.

Reputations are challenged because of falsehoods and unsustainable relationships. There is only a bankrupt moral proposition left on the table, waiting for the influencers to serve a "Jesus feast" for the sake of career ascension. It is the notion of appearance without substance.

In the heavy mantle of salesmanship, a dance ensues – a delicate waltz across the teetering edge of human psychology. Without the notes or structure of academia. Let's not fool each other. Sales is a challenging profession. We are tasked with understanding human behavior and asked to apply insights that are both real and credible. We need to connect with strangers and build a relationship, almost within a minute. This newfound friendship is then expected to translate into financial rewards, based on our assurances that our product will bring significant value to the client's bottom line. Every day we compete with ourselves and others in the ever-changing landscape of a bottomless market. It's demanding, and many choose to leave the profession as the odds of success can be daunting. However, sales can be a fulfilling career if you embrace self-motivation and innovation, creative thinking and planning and continuous learning. Be open to new ideas, be engaging, be courageous and let the market guide you. You'll know what steps to take.

Be an alchemist of opportunity, forge bonds and flourish.

The End.

ACKNOWLEDGEMENT

The most poignant question arises: who deserves our deepest acknowledgment in a career that traversed numerous countries and sparked countless conversations about business, particularly in the realm of media sales? Honestly, I wouldn't be writing this book without the humbling experiences I encountered along the way—moments intertwined with those who seemed inept, the underwhelming, and the boastful. They adorned themselves in a facade of pride, ego, and branded clothing that belonged to others, creating a stark contrast to the essence of genuine leadership.

This journey illuminated for me the divide between diligent, dedicated leaders and those who barely show up, often lost in a whirlwind of confusion, managing through charisma rather than competence. It's almost comical how some seek refuge on boards, aligning themselves with fellow travelers who merely scrape by, hitching rides to the next boardroom meeting on the success of others' hard work.

Yet, amid the clamor of self-aggrandizement and superficiality, it is the steady, serious workers—the quiet achievers—who truly deserve our recognition. These are the individuals who persistently labor in the shadows, navigating the noise of Jackals and grinning apes that dominate the spotlight. This book is dedicated to them, with hopes of offering a moral map for survival in a world that often seems skewed against the earnest.

May their stories and efforts be acknowledged, and may this journey inspire them to embrace their value and potential. Their unwavering commitment is what truly shapes the future, and it is time we shine a light on their contributions.

www.ingramcontent.com/pod-product-compliance
Lightning Source LLC
Chambersburg PA
CBHW011729020426
42333CB00024B/2803